The Grin Gal's Guide to Waiting

YOUR LIFE
on HOLD
Don't Hate the Wait

Kathy Carlton Willis

3G BOOKS

Your Life on Hold: Don't Hate the Wait
©2022 by Kathy Carlton Willis
www.kathycarltonwillis.com

ISBN-13: 978-1-7330728-8-5

Published by 3G Books, Jasper, TX 75951

Editing, interior, and cover design by Michelle Rayburn www.missionandmedia.com

Your Life on Hold will inspire anyone sitting in life's waiting room. It reminds me again of why we think of Kathy as God's grin gal! I was drawn into the topic because I've had my own on-hold moments when it seemed like life wasn't taking me where I wanted to go. If you're feeling stuck or frustrated by delays not of your own doing, the book will help you hold on during the on-hold moments. Kathy shows how God adds meaning to our lives in the meantime while we wait for our "next" to happen. I especially like the PAUSE acronym and steps at the end of each chapter. I can't wait for my girlfriends to get a hold of this book!

–**Tara Royer Steele**, author of *Eat. Pie. Love.* Owner of Royers Pie Haven and All Things Acres, gatherer of people and Jesus over pie, tararoyersteele.com

Kathy Carlton Willis has done it again with her newest resource, *Your Life on Hold.* She gently challenges Christians to lean in hard to our heavenly Father when we are faced with difficulties. A seasoned sufferer herself, Kathy shares her own struggles (and they are daunting, to be sure) and how she finds comfort and strength in the truths of God's Word. The author guides readers to share their points of pain with the Lord and then implement the PAUSE method . . . read it to discover how powerful these action steps are. Kathy's book is a keeper and a repeat read. Buy one for yourself and for your family and friends who are struggling in their own waiting rooms.

–**Michele Howe**, reviewer, columnist, author of 28 books, including the newly released *Grace & Gratitude for Everyday Life,* michelehowe.wordpress.com

Who enjoys waiting? Nobody I know! What if someone offered a strategy to make those times productive, even meaningful? In *Your Life on Hold,* Kathy encourages a change of perspective—believing God has a purpose in what seems a delay, trusting him to use it for his greater good, and making the most of those baffling stretches when nothing seems to be happening. She shares the hard-learned truth that when we see waiting as a gift, it allows us to grow. Each chapter ends with suggestions for handling the pause: Pray, Adjust, Undertake, Seek, Evaluate. Kathy writes, "What we *learn* during the pause is as productive as what we *do* in the remainder of the journey." If you're feeling stuck, this book will renew your hope and ignite a spirit of adventure!

–**Dianne Barker,** speaker, radio host, multi-book author, including *I Don't Chase the Garbage Truck down the Street in My Bathrobe Anymore!* diannebarker.com

In *Your Life on Hold*, Kathy Carlton Willis has written a practical, spiritual guide on waiting. With transparency and humor, she offers personal and biblical examples of overwhelming situations when waiting can leave us wondering what God is doing. Kathy also uses biblical truths and powerful principles to help us renew our joy and purpose during any life pause. Kathy presents not platitudes but positive attitudes that will encourage you to embrace the wait and bring you full circle to the bigness of God.

–**Rebecca Barlow Jordan**, bestselling inspirational author of
13 books, including award-winning *Day-votions* with
Your Faithful Father, rebeccabarlowjordan.com

Your Life on Hold offers encouragement for those sitting in life's waiting room. If you're feeling stuck in a story you didn't choose, you know the pain and impatience of waiting for it to all work out. Author Kathy Carlton Willis has been there and is still there—experiencing a revolving door of waiting rooms! With her trademark humor and biblical insights, she will speak hope into your struggle. Rest in God's presence and peace as you wait.

–**Michelle Diercks**, Bible teacher, speaker, host of the Peace in
His Presence podcast, author of *Promised Rest: Finding Peace
in God's Presence,* michellediercks.com

I've known Kathy for years and can attest that she is well-versed in living a life on hold. Because God doesn't waste anything, we are blessed with this excellent resource for individual use or group study. Kathy's writing is real and relatable. You'll understand right away that she gets it. Not only does her book offer inspiration, encouragement, and empathy, but it's also loaded with helpful ideas and aha! moments. And speaking of aha! moments . . . after spending a few moments with Kathy, you'll come away realizing that God can actually use those not-so-fun pauses in life for your good and the good of others. If you're tired of waiting, waiting, waiting, I highly recommend you read *Your Life on Hold*.

–**Twila Belk** (aka The Gotta Tell Somebody Gal), writer,
speaker, author of *Raindrops from Heaven* and
The Power to Be, gottatellsomebody.com

Kathy's new book, *Your Life on Hold,* reminds me of how God has been here in all my painful yet hopeful waiting times, just as surely as when I am actively going and doing. Learning that life happens along the journey more than at the destination remains an ongoing process. I related to the author's frustrations, questions, and emotions. I've wandered and wondered through similar valleys, especially with several life-threatening conditions that completely stalled my ability to live normally. Kathy's comforting and inspiring words brought me to tears, to a renewed sense of hope, and ultimately into a closer walk with my Lord. Waiting can be a wonderful station along this journey of life, especially when he is with us in the wait.

–**Jill Marie Thomas**, business owner, teacher, speaker, multi-book author including Redemption Rental Series, jillmariethomas.com

Enduring a season of waiting is difficult. We want answers. We've become so accustomed to quick . . . fast . . . now that many of our patience muscles have lost their flexibility. Within the pages of Kathy's book, *Your Life on Hold,* you will find wonderful lessons that help rebuild that muscle through exercise again. Kathy's wisdom, insight, and complete vulnerability provide her readers with scriptural, relatable, and sometimes even giggle-worthy connection. (I found something within every chapter I could relate to!) Perhaps if we were to follow her advice to PAUSE, we would more eagerly embrace our seasons of waiting because it is within the pause that God reveals more of himself to us.

–**Kolleen Lucariello**, author of *#beYOU: Change Your Identity One Letter at a Time* and co-director of Activ8Her.Inc., speakkolleen.com

Kathy Carlton Willis has penned a book just for me. Her words of comfort for the in-between time of waiting on God's timing provide a soothing balm for the weary heart. *Your Life on Hold* coaches me on how to be still in God's waiting room when I would rather rush his response. And Kathy provides practical steps for turning the wait into a productive lesson in patience, perseverance, and pursuing God. This book is a hands-on resource for all who wonder if God hears when life comes to a halt.

–**Sally Ferguson**, reviewer, caregiver, encourager, pastor's wife, women's ministry leader, and author of *How to Plan a Women's Retreat Playbook,* sallyferguson.net

Challenged by her own waiting room situations, Kathy Carlton Willis shares the prescription for grin-gal living, even when the season is long, uncertain, or unfair. *Your Life on Hold* encompasses so many of the scenarios I have found myself impatiently waiting through. Kathy covers them all with her grin-gal style of humor, encouragement, and biblical study. She doesn't want you to just survive the waiting experience—she wants you to thrive while learning and growing in your walk with God. Consider her your personal cheerleader as you read through each chapter—chapters that will leave you nodding your head in agreement. As an expert waiter, she's used moment after moment—otherwise wasted in the waiting room—and reclaimed them for God's purpose.

–**Gina Stinson**, teacher, pastor's wife, devotional storyteller, and author of *Reclaimed: The Stories of Rescued Moments and Days,* ginastinson.com

I've seen Kathy brave several waiting-room seasons in her life and still radiate God's joy through that effervescent grin. *Your Life on Hold* addresses those life-on-pause situations through a biblical lens while offering practical application. You'll laugh out loud at her honest inner monologue, relate to ALL the feelings of being on hold, and be inspired to find meaningful moments during the wait. Read the book on your own or join up with a friend or small group. Waiting is always better when shared with fellow waiters.

–**Tammy Anderud**, administration pastor, Praise Church, adoptive mom, and former director of surgical nursing

Using true-to-form wit and joy, Kathy brings enlightenment to the subject that my client widows and I struggle with daily—life on hold. We wanna "hate the wait." By revealing her humanness, Kathy encourages us to give ourselves grace when our thoughts seem self-centered and demanding. She shines a light on a re-frame from God's Word that stirs the soul to see his wisdom. She gently prods us to be open to the possibility that there just might be another perspective, that we might grow during the process, and it will get better than this. Life's circumstances don't have to dictate our emotional life. *Your Life on Hold* demonstrates how when we choose the joy of the Lord versus defaulting to our human reactions, we can experience peace that surpasses our own understanding.

–**Pam Stoddard**, life coach and widow survivor, lifelong joy chaser, owner and coach of Choosing Joy after Grief and Loss coaching programs, pamstoddard.com

CONTENTS

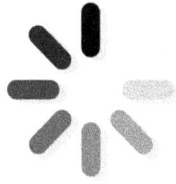

INTRODUCTION

P robably the hardest thing for me, and most of you, is the trial of hurry up and wait. Left unchecked, it tests my patience, challenges my contentment, and sours my joy. If you are in a season not of your own choosing, you might find yourself wishing for something different or more. Answers or solutions.

From My Heart to Yours

The middle of your mess might look different than mine. But it is pressing on you. You might be fighting worry storms and inescapable frustrations. Burdens that weigh down rather than lift off. Is something making you feel as if your "next" is postponed or delayed? A circumstance that is draining your joy? This book will help you find peace and contentment while you wait for life to improve or change. You will gain new tools to make the most of today while waiting for the hopes of tomorrow to be fulfilled.

Some of you are going through problems that go deeper than what I can touch on in the book. I encourage those with struggles that hinder their quality of life or activities of daily living to seek professional help. In the back of the book, there's a resource section where I list some possible times to seek help. It's important for me to mention right up front that I'm not saying I have all the answers!

I'm also not saying that if you have enough faith or patience, you won't be affected by the trials of waiting. There's no easy button when it comes to these tough seasons.

> *So the Lord must wait for you to come to him so he can show you his love and compassion. For the Lord is a faithful God. Blessed are those who wait for his help.*
> (Isaiah 30:18)

Personal Trials of Waiting

I've been writing this book for over ten years. And evidently, God is allowing me to have plenty of experience and writing material! I've faced one circumstance after another. I'm sure you understand the nature of these waiting periods. I anticipate a great end to a trying situation, only to have that hope thwarted by another setback. Here are a few of the detours I've faced going back even before I started writing this project. I'm redeeming the unpleasant circumstances by declaring it fodder for the book!

> The hardest thing is the trial of hurry up and wait.

- **Deconditioning/reconditioning revolving door.** I gradually built up from being disabled to being able to walk at a fast pace for an hour. Only to be put in the hospital for a lung infection that went septic into my bloodstream. After ten days in the hospital, I required a walker to get to the restroom. The rebuilding process started all over again.

- **Deflating rejection of the professional kind.** Three different publishers offered book contracts and then didn't deliver. One dropped off the face of the earth with zero communication. Then they didn't publish the book they rush ordered—even though I scrambled to submit the manuscript on time. One publisher delayed books two and three of our series deal despite having it all set up and promoted. Then they canceled the contract. And a different publisher closed her doors. Two books were published but then dead in the water.

- **Near-death experience.** The risky medication with the black box warning started to help my autoimmune disease. Until it didn't. That landed me in the hospital with a wiped-out immune system—my immune system had nothing left to fight a raging infection. Waiting for healing made me lean into God for support.

- **Disappointing letdowns.** The acquaintance who said she'd help me with a special project ended up flaking on me and dropped the entire thing in my lap. Not only did she break her commitment, but she also lost out on a source of income—which made no sense. Figuring out how to do it at the last minute wasn't like ground zero. It was like ground minus twelve. Other friends decided to not attend my big ministry event. I had been there for them. It was my time, right? I waited. They didn't show.

- **Unmet family dreams.** I couldn't bear children of my own, and five adoption opportunities fell through. The wait felt unbearable too. Heartbreaking doesn't begin to explain the level of pain.

- **Over-promised and under-delivered.** After great expense and delays in getting to a famous medical center for a ten-day evaluation, the team assigned to my case didn't meet and didn't address several of the issues, sending me home with instructions to use over-the-counter acetaminophen. They missed diagnosing thyroid cancer, ankylosing spondylitis, primary immune deficiency, and Eagle syndrome.

- **So many more.** I'll share some of my waiting room stories throughout the book.

Your Waiting Room

You've endured your own pauses and delays. When I asked my beta readers to share their stories, we discovered some common themes. I'm certain you'll relate to several of these waiting scenarios.

1. Job stress or joblessness, along with financial needs.
2. Unanswered prayers and feeling directionless.
3. Medical trials and health struggles.
4. Housing issues or homelessness.
5. Feeling stuck in a season or rut.
6. Family or friendship struggles.
7. Church hurts and conflicts.
8. Purpose questioned along with closed doors.
9. Emotional and mental burdens.
10. Feeling invisible, isolated, or misunderstood.
11. Depression and discouragement.
12. Solutions outside your control.

I am praying for you as you wait for God to provide the next step to your answer—it isn't easy to be patient! As you read this book, take it at a slow enough pace so you can absorb the content without adding to your sense of overwhelm. Give yourself permission to breathe.

My Life Delayed

I have several God-and-me times yearly to evaluate the priorities he wants me to have, the goals he sets for me—you name it. The frustrating part comes when I think I have my marching orders from God, and then something comes into my life that puts everything on hold. I get so antsy to want to rush into action—to do what God has planted as a burning passion in my life. Instead, I have no choice but to wait. It feels like I'm expected to sit on my hands! I'm quite certain you can relate.

I've come to realize that I hate the wait because it practically drives me crazy to feel like I'm not making progress. And I've been programmed to think I have to be *doing* something or see a situation moving in the right direction to count as progress. I'm learning from back-to-back-to-back on-hold circumstances that it's in the wait where we grow, others grow, and conditions come together for a better outcome later on. Just because we can't see the signs of progress doesn't mean nothing good is going on.

The wait is not a delay. It's an on-purpose plateau to let what *used to be* catch up with what's *going to be* in the future. It's just like losing

> Just because we can't see the signs of progress doesn't mean nothing good is going on.

weight. If we don't allow for the plateaus when we diet, our skin doesn't shrink up, and we walk around like Shar Pei puppies. We don't want saggy, baggy skin, and we don't want saggy, baggy lives, either. A life on hold isn't a life delayed. It's simply not time yet.

What do you do about it when you hit a delay in your git-up-and-go? Does it derail you? Do you learn to be flexible? How do you cope? After you are no longer on hold, does hindsight help you find the blessing in the wait? Perhaps you recognize a drama avoided by the delay or a travesty missed by the trial of waiting. Or maybe you see the results of a spiritual growth spurt that took place during the time you felt stalled out.

Do you get sleepy listening to on-hold music while waiting for the intended party to come on the phone? I always feel like nodding off. It has the same effect as eating turkey. Naptime! I wonder if on-hold situations cause that same sleepy feeling. No wonder we don't like it!

During a prior holding pattern, I had an aha! moment. I felt as if the Lord was asking me, "What attitude adjustment can you make today to help you get closer to the future I've dreamed up just for you?" I had been so focused on health challenges that the goals God placed into my heart seemed back-burnered. Each discouraging bit of news or frustrating wait caused me to get further and further away from the joy of living out those God-given dreams. I'm happiest when I'm working in my strengths, not handcuffed by my weaknesses.

One thing that came out of my waiting seasons is content for this book. God is an expert up-cycler. He takes some part of our lives that we think is useless or wasted and recycles it into something better—more meaningful. Beautiful, even. If my life on hold can be used to encourage or minister to someone else, it is worth it.

I've learned to use these pauses for evaluation. What do I do that drains me? What energizes me? God loves for us to accentuate those things that propel us rather than those that drag us down. Motors, not anchors. Of course, all work has aspects we don't like—that's why it's called work. But it's important to do something daily that gets us jazzed. Can you put your finger on that thing that makes your motor purr?

> Let's accentuate the things that propel us rather than those things that drag us down. Motors, not anchors.

Part of transitioning out of the wait is to anticipate something new.

Join me today by asking yourself, "What attitude adjustment can I make today to help me get closer to the future God's dreamed up just for me?"

Small Groups, Bible Studies, and Book Clubs

This book is ideal for small group or Bible study discussion. On the kick-off week, you could read the introduction together and have a casual gathering to interact and break the ice. If you cover five chapters a week for the remaining weeks, you end up with a six-week program. The chapters are short enough to read one in a single sitting. I'm available to visit your group via video call for the first or last week of the study and can provide leader helps if you contact me.

About the Book

Each chapter is designed to be a short reading session since most people experiencing life on hold have a hard time focusing on longer chapters. We need a bit of inspiration, a heartwarming or funny real-life story, a little motivation—some empathy. You'll get all that in each chapter of *Your Life on Hold*.

Sometimes when you're going through a lull, it's difficult to want to read advice or hear about someone else's experiences. It comes across as if they don't have a clue what you're going through. Yet they try to say they can relate because of their own challenges—offering empathy. But it feels all wrong. Like a competition to see who has the most pitiful life. I hope you'll find this book different—refreshing—giving you a new way to see life without it being more *blah-blah-blah* rambling.

At the end of each chapter is a takeaway section set up to help you make tangible progress while you feel like you're treading water. I use the acronym PAUSE. The section is called "During the PAUSE."

P–Pray
A–Adjust
U–Undertake
S–Seek
E–Evaluate

> I will look for God's presence, provision, and peace as I withstand this pause.

It will include a prayer to use when you don't know what to pray, an adjustment to make, an action to undertake, something to seek, and a situation to evaluate. You might not have the energy to tackle all of these. However, make a good attempt to work on at least one of these objectives during the pause. You'll find doing even just one step of PAUSE will help you not feel so stuck or in a funk. You can learn not to hate the wait—just as I did.

You'll notice all of the PAUSE statements after the prayer are

"I will" phrases. I have found that making intentional statements gives extra determination to really get them done. If we use "I hope to," "I'll try," or "If nothing gets in the way" type statements, we're already creating loopholes for failure. Of course, we know anything we do in life is conditional on other situations outside our control, but the PAUSE statements deal with what *is* in our control.

Following PAUSE, I include a notable quote attributed to a public figure. They provide inspiration and wisdom. Following that is a quote from me as if you caught me in the raw—in the weakness that can dominate on-hold lives. Perhaps you'll relate to these admissions from the dark side of on-holdedness. (I mean no disrespect to the original quotes or people quoted—I'm just being real.) My "in the raw" responses are often humorous (or maybe even a bit snarky), a typical coping skill when the wait seems unbearable. And finally, I include a quote from me as I look at that same concept through Christ, as his Spirit rules and reigns in my life.

Seeing the progression is one way to be motivated to have similar steps toward victory in your own life. Adopt a sense of adventure. Ask, "What's coming next?" Instead of that question being a pessimistic take on how the negative news is piling up in your life, ask it with anticipation of something good just around the corner.

During the PAUSE

Pray

Father, as I read this book, help me to grow in patience so that I might endure what you have for me during the wait. Download fresh contentment and, yes—even joy!

Adjust

I will adjust my attitude so it will evolve from snarky and discontented to joyful and peace filled.

Undertake

I will make use of this silent interval rather than waiting for an open door to see progress.

Seek

I will look for God's presence, provision, and peace as I withstand this pause.

Evaluate

I will evaluate what I hate about the wait so I can learn to let go of the resentment.

QUOTE: "When it grows dark enough, we can see stars." –Charles A. Beard[1]

ME in the RAW: The darkness feels more like someone slammed the coffin lid down on top of me rather than sitting in the dark of a beautiful planetarium!

ME in the SPIRIT: God's light is bright enough to not only illuminate my dark space but to warm my tepid life.

Chapter One

HARD TO HOLD IT

I f you ever had that gotta go, gotta go problem, and you hear your mother's voice asking why you didn't go before you left home, then you know how hard it is to hold it. What is "it," and why do we have to hold it while we wait? Evaluate what you tend to cling to during the trial of delays and see what changes when you are content to hold on to God alone.

Toddler Candy Challenge

Have you seen the toddler candy challenge on social media and *America's Funniest Home Videos*? It's funny to see the kids' responses when instructed they will get to eat the candy sitting in front of them if they wait until the parent's return. Then Mom or Dad leaves the room while the video continues. Some of the children struggle with the wait, others cheat and gobble up the candy, and others are prideful in their ability to obey their parents.

It made me think of how I am when I'm asked to wait for something. I can envision it right in front of me—that elusive answer or remedy or goal. And it seems as if others are sitting there waiting right along with me for their version of life candy.

The cheater who eats the candy while his parent is gone seems instantly happy. Immediate gratification. The waiter looks tortured. The wait is so hard! The children who wait are deemed more intelligent. They can see the benefit of waiting. That forward-sight informs their self-control.

> What do you hold on to when the way is rough?

There's another version of it with two dogs and dog treats. One dog is obedient and waits to be told to eat the treat. Wait for it. Wait for it. He waits. So patient. Confident Daddy will soon say, "Eat it!" But another dog comes right up and eats the treat the other dog is waiting for. The first dog looks as if he's saying, "Hey, I was being good. Then you just come along and get the very thing I'm waiting for. You didn't follow the rules!"

How do you feel during the wait when you're trying to do all the right things, and it seems like someone else gets what you're waiting for, and you're left waiting? In the end, the ones who looked happiest were those who waited for the prize, and their Daddy eventually gave them what they waited for. They had the joy of the desired outcome and the joy of trusting Daddy in the wait and doing what he wanted.

Hold On

Sometimes, the only way we will learn a new way is to hold on to something familiar while not allowing ourselves to focus on what could go wrong. That reminds me of my brother. He was a late bloomer when it came to walking. He pulled himself up to the furniture but didn't step away—he held on tight. He felt safest clinging to Mommy or Daddy or sitting securely on his bottom. But then came along an oversized plastic golf club. This toy gave him plenty of security. He held on to it and actually toddled a few steps, thinking the club was connected to the ground. From what

I've heard (I was a mere preschooler myself), the steps weren't pretty, but they got the job done. It was the first time he felt safe to go from one point to another on his own two feet.

Aren't we the same way? We often must cling to our security blanket to try something new, walk in unfamiliar territory, or manage to avoid the obstacles and detours in order to get to our destination. What do you hold on to when the way is rough?

The word *hold* has been on my mind a lot during this recent waiting period. It means so much when it comes to feeling a bit stuck—floundering. First, I feel *on hold* (which is how I got the subtitle for the book). You know how it is when you try to get through to someone on the phone, and the receptionist puts you on hold? You wait, listen to drowsy music, watch the clock, wait some more, and maybe if all goes well, you'll finally get to talk to the intended party. Being on hold is no fun. It seems like it accomplishes nothing measurable—a waste of time.

Another use of the word *hold* reminds me of what I'm holding on to when I'm going through a rough patch. To whom or what do I cling? Often, you can check your sent email to see who you yammer to the most about your problems. Or outgoing calls or texts. Venting on social media to whoever will listen. Or, if it's an object rather than a person that acts as a security blanket, you can look at your checkbook and receipts to see what you run to when life is tough.

The word *hold* has one more important use when it comes to being stuck in the middle. In this instance, I'm referring

> God's hands mean a lot. It's the support we need most, the embrace we crave most, and the security we miss most.

to what it's like to know God is holding on to us when we feel like we've lost our grip. God never loses his grasp on us. One of my favorite childhood hymns was "He's Got the Whole World in His Hands." There are current renditions of it that make the lyrics really stick in my mind. God's hands made us, made the world we live in, and paid the price on the cross for our salvation. They welcome us into his presence. Those hands mean a lot. It's the support we need most, the embrace we crave most, and the security we miss most.

It's comforting to know that when I'm on hold and feel like I'm losing my grip, God has me in his strong grasp.

> *My sheep listen to my voice; I know them, and they follow me. I give them eternal life, and they will never perish. No one can snatch them away from me, for my Father has given them to me, and he is more powerful than anyone else. No one can snatch them from the Father's hand. The Father and I are one.*
>
> (John 10:27–30)

One Ringy Dingy

Lily Tomlin played Ernestine, the telephone operator on the 1960s TV show *Rowan & Martin's Laugh-In*. She famously started her skits with, "One ringy dingy . . . two ringy dingy." She spoke through her nose and frequently asked, "Have I reached the party to whom I am speaking?" I recall her working at the switchboard and placing the caller on hold or dropping the call if it pleased her fancy. Lily Tomlin was quite hilarious in this role, but can you imagine if her character were real? We wouldn't be much of a fan of Ernestine. In fact, she would grate on my last nerve!

I simply do not like being placed on hold, even though, in my previous line of work, I often had to put others on hold in order to serve everyone in the best way possible. When I placed someone on hold, there was good reason. If someone was ahead of them in the queue, I needed to deal with that person first. If the person on hold made a request or asked a question to which I had to hunt down the answer, placing them on hold was necessary.

Those same guidelines for receptionists apply to our lives when we're on hold. When God allows us to be on hold, perhaps he's working in someone else's life. Not that they matter more, but because their timeline needs to be addressed before it intersects with our timeline—to work out the ultimate plan for all involved. Sure, he is God and can work on multiple answers to prayer at once, but sometimes we get placed on hold for all the other details to fall into place. Maybe I'm on hold so God can work out the details I'm so eagerly waiting to see revealed. The on-hold moment isn't a delay. It means something else is going on behind the scenes to get me to the place where I can be connected to my call.

Plus, there are situations that aren't God's fault when we are placed on hold or have something similar to a dropped call. God allows us the grace space to make mistakes. This next part gets deep, and I don't even pretend to understand it completely. God has sovereign control—yes. But he often allows us to make choices outside of his best desires for us. He will redeem these problems, but the issue isn't always something he initiated—he simply picks up the pieces broken by a human who has imperfect future-sight. In other words, there are people in our lives like Ernestine, and we have a delay because of their mistakes.

> It boils down to holding on tighter to God and letting him decide what needs to be in my life and what needs to disappear.

I don't like it much when someone puts me on hold, but I wait it out because I know it will get to the desired outcome. Do I wait with that same positive expectancy when it seems my life is on hold? Or would I prefer to have a chat with Ernestine and try to convince her to pull all the lines out of the switchboard so I get bumped up to next in line?

> *Listen to my voice in the morning, Lord. Each morning*
> *I bring my requests to you and wait expectantly.*
> (Psalm 5:3)

> God, help me exchange those lifesavers for the One who truly saves my life.

What's in Your Hand?

When I think of the story I shared earlier about my brother holding the toy golf club, it reminds me of the biblical account about Moses in Exodus when God asked him, *"What is that in your hand?"** If God asked me what I was holding on to, my answer would probably reflect some good things and some not-so-good things. How would you answer? Here are some of the common ones:

- Faith
- Hope
- Expectations
- Duties
- Goals
- Disappointments
- Doubts
- Past accomplishments
- Baggage
- Self-sufficiency
- Trust

As I process this list, I'm asking God to show me what I need to let go of and what I need to hold tighter to. Really it boils down to holding on tighter to him and letting him decide what needs to be in my life and what needs to disappear.

Often when I begin to resent a waiting period, it's because I'm holding too tightly to a certain desired outcome, and I'm not

---

* Exodus 4:2

16

flexible enough to be okay with a different solution. Do I get in the way of what is best because I'm only looking for one open door?

What if I let go of it and expect the unexpected? I open myself up to letting God surprise me.

Much of the time, I think it is up to me to hold tight, but when I try to do things in my own power, I mess it all up!

I think of the illustration (oldie but goodie) that tells how to trap a monkey by putting food in a hollowed-out coconut. Create a hole big enough for the empty hand to go in but too small for the full hand to come out. The monkey is essentially trapped because he's holding on to something. What is trapping me because I won't let go? Surrender is opening my hand and releasing it so I can hold on to God.

During the PAUSE

Pray

Father, I want to let go of this security blanket so I hold tightly to you alone. Show me what I go to as my "little saviors." Help me exchange those lifesavers for the One who truly saves my life.

Adjust

I will surrender my idols (the things I prioritize in front of God) and leave them at the altar of my heart.

Undertake

I will spend more time with God in prayer. I will go to him *first* when I'm having a hard time holding it together.

Seek

I will find a new reminder to go to God during a trying situation. I will use that visual cue as an alert to pray or meditate. (Example: Pick a mindless activity I do several times a day, such as brushing my teeth or getting a drink of water.)

Evaluate

I will look at my messages and see who I'm going to when I need to vent or when I seek to be rescued. Next time I reach for that security blanket, I will use it as a prompt to talk to God first.

> **QUOTE:** "The happiest people I know are the ones who have learned how to hold everything loosely and have given the worrisome, stress-filled, fearful details of their lives into God's keeping." –Chuck Swindoll[2]
>
> **ME in the RAW:** I thought I was supposed to hold on. You mean I'm supposed to let go? Which is it?
>
> **ME in the SPIRIT:** Lord, I'm letting go now. I'm holding on to you alone. And I'm trusting in the fact that you are holding on to me.

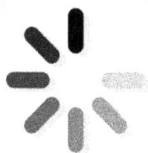

Chapter Two

LEARNING IN THE WAIT

G od doesn't waste any of our pain, and we need to adopt that
same mindset. What can we learn during this waiting period? Sometimes the wait wears us out too much to concentrate on
much of anything—let alone learn something new. How can we
make the best of this holding pattern? By being alert to life, we can
grow even when it seems like we're not getting anywhere.

Learn Your Lesson!

Growing up, I was a corner camper. Yes, my mother's chosen discipline style often included placement of the errant child (that
would be me) in the nearest corner. The precursor to a time-out,
but with a lot more humiliation involved. Mom was a smart cook-
ie (still is). She knew I needed to slow down long enough to make
a correction in my behavior. But what she said as she placed me
in the corner stuck with me. "You're going in a corner so you can
learn your lesson."

I admit, in the first bit of time with the walls tickling my nose,
all I could think of was whatever fun time I was missing out on.
I wasn't thinking about what I was supposed to learn, let alone

determining to correct my behavior. But I knew I didn't like being taken out of action. Slowing me down was an appropriate punishment for this girl missing first gear. Often the only lesson I learned was that I didn't like standing in a corner, so whatever I did to get there, I didn't want to do it again.

When we go through tough on-hold spells, we aren't sure *what* we're supposed to learn, but we feel that the quicker we learn it, the quicker we might get out of the holding pattern.

> *The Lord says, "I will guide you along the best pathway for your life. I will advise you and watch over you."*
> (Psalm 32:8)

> *Take my yoke upon you. Let me teach you, because I am humble and gentle at heart, and you will find rest for your souls. For my yoke is easy to bear, and the burden I give you is light."*
> (Matthew 11:29–30)

What will God teach you during this pause?

Life Lessons

I've had a full house of waiting rooms. In those seasons, life feels on hold. One of the frequent flyers of holding patterns is my health (or lack thereof!). At my worst, in addition to physical symptoms, my mind feels fuzzy, my energy sags, and I lack direction.

While medical challenges are pretty tough to deal with, one of my worst on-hold trials happened during a full year of waiting to see how God would provide when my husband was out of work. He applied for over one hundred jobs. After selling all our collectibles, we weren't sure how we would keep from financial doom. We learned what it meant to rely on food stamps and now have greater compassion toward anyone going through the holding pattern of joblessness.

They say hindsight is 20/20—perspective brings everything into focus. But I say future-sight is 20/20—it provides a perspective of hope and heaven. Even though the here and now is stinky, the future looks bright when we anticipate joining the Father in his abode. I tell myself frequently, *This is temporary!* Adopting future-sight is a wonderful coping skill for us waiting-room dwellers.

During one of my holding patterns, people kept asking me what God was teaching me. My first reaction to that question (keep in mind, I was still in the middle of it and didn't have the benefit of stability) was, "Am I supposed to be learning? You mean I have to endure all this *and* pay attention? I don't have the energy or focus for that."

> By being alert to life, we can grow even when it seems like we're not getting anywhere.

I couldn't put one more ounce of oomph into any sort of growth. All I experienced was the presence of God. He was right there with me. It reminded me of the times Dad would drive us down to the riverfront, and we sat on the retaining wall at the edge of the Mississippi River. Dad was right there with me, but we didn't talk. We just looked out at that long river. We could look north toward Hannibal and see where the river came from. And we could look the other direction and see it flow toward St. Louis. We didn't have to say anything, but it meant a lot that we had that time together. Nothing mattered other than that we shared that experience.

Now I can look back on recent on-hold moments and realize the lesson I was supposed to learn was that God's presence is enough.

It Isn't about Me

I learned that often those times I wait aren't about me. Maybe someone needs the benefit of the experience to overcome a struggle or to grow in spiritual maturity. We aren't alone when it seems we're on hold—others are affected, others are watching, and others have the opportunity to gain something from our experience. So, it isn't simply about me.

I already knew it wasn't about me when it came to worship stuff, life stuff, everyday stuff, attitude stuff. I knew it for setting priorities, goals, and even wishes.

But as I prayed in a recent life-on-hold waiting period, my heart heard God clearly say, *This isn't about you,* regarding my medical journey. The setbacks I experienced with doctors and treatments and diagnosis and side effects and black box warnings that became a reality weren't to grow me. (Yet I do grow from my health struggles.) The circumstances weren't there to chastise me— although it's always good to turn from bad habits and patterns when God corrects our steps.

But the primary reason for these seeming setbacks was for the benefit of someone else—maybe not just *one* someone else. God let me in on the secret that it wasn't about me. And somehow, having that knowledge helped me hold on when I was on hold—knowing God was holding me. God isn't out to get (zap) you, but he is out to get (hold) you! Does it help to know that?

> God isn't out to get (zap) you, but he is out to get (hold) you!

So, if it's for the benefit of someone else—for their growth—for them to draw closer to God . . . how do I need to act so they best witness the Father in this? How can I make sure this experience leads them to praise him and want to be with him? When this happens, the effect is multiplied as they live it out with their sphere of influence.

I don't want my negative actions or attitudes to rub off on someone else and cause them to go down the wrong path. It would devastate me to think I led anyone astray. Do I have enough already built up inside of me to respond correctly during a trying time? Those spiritual instincts come from time with the

Father and being in his Word—from allowing the fruit of the Spirit to flow through me. We need to have this in reserve because we typically don't have any extra energy or focus available during a holding pattern.

Don't forget where these reserves are when you need them. The fuel is available ahead of time for when you need it. It stores everything you've saved up from your time with the Father to use on auto-pilot while you sort things out. And if you haven't had a close relationship with God before now, use this time to get close with him rather than figuring out how to get out of the holding pattern. It's more about hanging out with him, not finding the escape button.

Just because your life is on hold and it seems as if nothing is moving forward, there are still actions to take while you wait. It's like sitting on the tarmac waiting for a runway to open up for departure. What can you do as you wait for the opportunity to get moving again?

> Just because your life is on hold and it seems like nothing is moving forward, there are still actions to take while you wait.

Asking Questions

My four-year-old buddy Ethan came for a visit. He hoisted a twenty-four case of Pepsi up to the doorstep for his friend Russ. So proud of his strength—grinning ear to ear because Pepsi is Russ's favorite beverage. We asked Ethan if he wanted to play with our twelve-week-old puppy, Mijo. I'm not sure if we offered so Mijo could get some exercise or to keep Ethan occupied so his dad and Russ could visit.

Ethan and I charged for the door to play with Mijo in the backyard. My little friend learned to play fetch almost as well as Mijo. Decidedly instant pals, Ethan proclaimed, "He Mijo, me Memo!" He was convinced Mijo liked him better than anyone else and that the puppy wanted to go home to live with him.

While in the backyard, a deluge of questions poured from Ethan's lips. "Why does Mijo chase the football?" "Where does he go to the bathroom?" And after he heard me cough, "How do we get sick?" I smiled to myself, as I could no longer keep count of the questions on both hands.

Occasionally it's easy to answer a child's questions, but sometimes even grown-ups don't know the answers. Often, adults tire of hearing a firing round of questions from little inquiring minds. Children learn by asking and ask by thinking. So, no matter how annoying excessive questioning might be, I enjoy a child who expands his mind with questions.

Christians don't always feel comfortable asking God questions. They are afraid it will sound as if they doubt God. Or perhaps they don't know how they will hear God's answer anyway, so why bother? We need to realize that, unlike us, God does have all the answers. At times, he knows it's best if we wait for the answer. Other times, he's thrilled to reveal to us what our hearts need to know.

> What matters to us, matters to God (because *we* matter to God).

Perhaps if we asked questions as freely as preschool children, God would bless our lack of inhibition with him. Sure, he might have to stifle a chuckle if we ask a question that seems trivial to him (in reality, they are all trivial compared to his infinite wisdom). Fortunately, what matters to us matters to God (because *we* matter to God).

God will answer as he sees fit and on his timetable. He might show you through his Word. Or possibly through the wisdom of another Christian. Sometimes God orchestrates circumstances to provide his response. Like Ethan, we never know unless we ask!

When You Have More Questions than Answers . . . Reframe the Questions

When we can't find answers to our questions, maybe we're asking the wrong questions. It's time to reframe the questions. Here are some questions we tend to ask, (Q) followed by examples of reframed questions (R).

Q: Why is this happening to me?
R: What does God want me to learn about him while I feel stuck?

Q: When will this be over?
R: What2 new focus do I need to concentrate on during this holding pattern?

Q: Why can't I catch a break?
R: How can God use this to align me closer to his purpose for my life?

Q: Why do others seem to have it easier than me?
R: How can God equip me through this time so I'm more comfortable with the next step?

Q: Why can't I be happy?
R: How can I find joy despite my circumstances?

Q: When will God answer my prayer?
R: Where in the Bible can I discover God's wisdom for this trial?

Q: How can I work up enough energy to deal with this?
R: What passion can I pursue that will energize me?

25

During the PAUSE

Pray

Father, help me to make the most of this waiting period. Show me what you would have me learn. Give me patience to endure the delays. Most of all, may I reflect you as I wait it out.

Adjust

I will recognize my self-pity attitudes and trade them for gratitude. This will rejuvenate me in the wait.

Undertake

I will dislodge being stuck in the pause rut by learning something new. Variety refreshes whatever feels stale.

Seek

I will look for someone else who is in a holding pattern and suggest we be encouragement buddies.

Evaluate

I will ask myself if there is any sin in my life that could be holding back God's hand of blessing, but I will not get bogged down in false guilt or condemnation since those are not of God.

QUOTE: "Patience is not the ability to wait, but how you act while you're waiting." –Joyce Meyer[3]

ME in the RAW: Why should I be patient? This is happening *to* me. I didn't ask for this!

ME in the SPIRIT: I can't work up patience on my own, but since it's a fruit of the Spirit, I can be equipped by the Original Source.

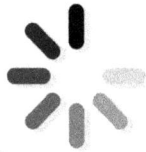

Chapter Three

HOLDING PATTERN OF WAITEDNESS

We've all experienced short periods when we feel like we're in a holding pattern. The plane keeps circling—when will it land so we can get to our destination? Sometimes these delays go on for much too long. How can we cope when we just want to get there already? By learning that life happens on the journey (including the pit stops) more than at the destination, we can embrace the wait.

A Stormy Night

As a women's event speaker, Mother's Day weekend has often meant extra traveling for me. I like it that way for lots of reasons. As a childless wife, Mother's Day can be a rough holiday for me. I've learned it works best to celebrate women and to stay busy. I'm genuine when I publicly recognize mothers and am grateful for the mom God gave me. So, it isn't a sad day—but I do have to focus my mindset in a better place.

One year, I flew Friday morning to speak for a women's banquet that night. Then the event planner rushed me back to the airport to catch the last flight out that evening. I needed to get to my next destination in time for a women's brunch the next day.

The afterglow of serving Christ at the banquet hadn't even sunk in yet. No time. I was in a hurry.

The wind was kicking up, but to be honest, I thought it was mostly from the speed of our vehicle cutting through the night. Then I noticed a few lightning bolts. Thunder. Big fat rain drops plopping on the windshield. The wipers swish-swished in beat to my heart, pulsing my silent plea that I make it on time.

In my hurry, I forgot my cane in the host's car. I navigated through the airport the best I could. Made it through security. As I rushed through the airport to my gate, I heard flights being canceled left and right. Whew! I made it to my gate, only to be confronted with a new trial.

> By learning that life happens on the journey (including the pit stops) more than at the destination, we can embrace the wait.

The flight was overbooked, and passengers from other flights had been combined with our passenger list. They took us in the order we checked in. By all rights, I shouldn't have made it on that plane because others had checked in before me to fill the plane's capacity. But somehow, someway (I know it was God), they called my name. I made it on the plane, and so did my luggage. I felt a little guilty that I was boarding and others were not. The last thing I heard as I walked down the jet bridge was their grumbles.

My assigned seat had been given to someone who checked in before me. The flight attendant seated me next to a young girl, flying solo, at the bulkhead. The front row was a blessing since I hobbled with a limp. I collapsed into my seat, thinking I could finally catch my breath, unwind, and relax after a crazy schedule. Time to get refreshed before my next speaking engagement. *Wrong.*

God had another assignment for me. The storm worsened, and the turbulence was horrific. The little girl next to me tensed up, and tears pooled in her eyes. We witnessed an incredible light show in the dark sky. The flight attendant made an announcement explaining why the seat belt sign was on. Just when I thought the storm couldn't get any more intense, it did. Then the pilot's voice came on to explain his difficult challenge of being rerouted to avoid the most severe storm—but he warned us that we would still experience a period of dangerous weather as he flew through the middle of the tempest.

The flight attendant was busy with others. So, it was up to me to calm the young passenger sitting to my right. I began to ask questions to get her talking. It was obvious my job was to keep her occupied so she wouldn't be overcome with fear—and when the plane dipped, to reassure her that it was okay to be frightened, but that we were in good hands.

You see, that holding pattern wasn't about me. It was about that little girl. It was about getting me to my speaking engagement in time to fulfill the purpose God had for me at that event. God made sure everything happened to get me there—even flying me in the middle of a storm when all other flights were canceled. I wasn't even supposed to have a seat on the plane, but there I was, smack dab in the middle of a holding pattern, witnessing God moments all around me. And, because I could see God's hand at work in getting me to that point, I could trust that he would get me the rest of the way. Landing gear dropping from the belly of the plane never sounded so good.

> It's in the *not knowing* that we learn the most.

Turbulent Holding Patterns

How is it possible a holding pattern is good for me? If waiting feels so bad, how can it be so good?

It's quite a dilemma when you recognize the signs of a holding pattern but don't have the ability to do anything about it. You know something is ending, but you're not quite sure what is next or where. You are willing to be yielded to God's plan, if only you knew what God's plan *was*. People try to act like it's so simple—you merely surrender to his will, and he directs you where to go. But sometimes, it's in the *not knowing* that we learn the most, so God allows us to stay in what feels like limbo for a while—what I call a "holding pattern of waitedness."

Following God's lead isn't always so cut and dried. Doors don't necessarily open when or where we expect.

In the waiting rooms of life, we are equipped for what lies ahead. We gain insights, stamina, vision, and passion. Then, when we hear our name called, we can step out in faith and walk toward our new thing.

Prepared in the Wait

Many wonder why it took the Israelites forty years to get to the promised land once they left bondage in Egypt. Perhaps the group needed that long for God to prepare his people. It isn't common to be equipped to go directly from dreaming a dream God has for us to realizing the accomplishment of that dream. In the middle is where it gets messy, but it's also where God is busy at work. It's where we see God show up. It's where a relationship with him means more than anything else. The destination is great, but oh the journey—the journey is where we meet with God!

We are a destination people—God is a journey God. It's not about the end goal; it's about the trip. God uses the wait to prepare us for the go.

Wilderness miracles:

- The Israelites crossed the unbridged Jordan with enemy armies chasing them. (God cleared the water and made a path on dry land.)[*]
- God provided manna and quail for sustenance.[†]
- Water gushed from a rock for the thirsty people to drink.[‡]

---

[*]   Exodus 14
[†]   Exodus 16
[‡]   Exodus 17; Numbers 20

- After Moses begged the Lord, God healed Miriam of leprosy.*

God redeemed what seemed like a delay or pause by bringing about some pretty amazing miracles in the wilderness. The Bible lists more than forty of them. What is God bringing about in your current holding pattern? Don't miss noticing the daily blessings due to your disappointment of not moving into that next desired season of life yet.

When Others Are Late

I hate waiting. Especially for others. It drives me crazy when I'm on time, but they're not. Their tardiness makes me feel as if they disrespect me somehow. I mean to be kind and understanding despite their lateness—to give the benefit of the doubt (what I call the benefit of grace). But sometimes, I grow impatient in the wait. Okay—*lots* of times, I grow impatient!

For most of my marriage, my husband was a pastor. That meant he was available to the congregation and the community 24/7. We aimed for a schedule, but having any sort of regular mealtime was laughable. He came home for lunch, but it was difficult to prepare it in advance since there was no way of knowing when he would be home until he actually arrived home. Even if he tried to shut down the computer right before noon to make it home, someone often caught him while he was on his way out of the office. The same thing happened at the end of day. Or when he did make it home on time, he frequently received phone calls that pulled him away from our plans. I learned to wait until I actually saw him to put our meal together. Slow-cooker and thirty-minute meals were great options.

> We are a destination people—God is a journey God.

I can't tell you the number of meals I burned, dried out, or

---

* Numbers 12

flopped before learning this lesson. I've never been good at this waiting thing.

A woman I know admits she is late on purpose. She says it takes the pressure off herself to not try to be on time. She doesn't realize how her delays cost her friends a great deal of inconvenience. And when we adjust our schedule to allow for her delays, it's still frustrating. Her lack of concern for how her tardiness affects us feels a lot like disrespect. But in actuality, she is not thinking of others. She is thinking of self. (Sound like a familiar frame of mind?)

I guess I've been waiting for people to be ready most of my life. When I was in junior high, I walked to school with a friend who always wanted me to be at her house at a certain time—I think it was something like 7:45 a.m. I'd get there, and she'd be just finishing up her soft-boiled egg, served with crumbled bacon over a broken-up piece of toast. From there, she'd go to the bathroom (telling me to follow her), where

> I will examine how serious my impatience is so I can deal with it before it turns to bitterness.

she used her Waterpik. Then she'd curl her bangs to get that feathered look everyone went for those days. All while I watched. I had her morning ritual down.

I'm not sure why I was so patient in those days. Are we given a dose of patience when we are born, and each time we wait on someone or something, we use up a little bit of that dose? Perhaps by the time we reach that magic age of fifty, we realize we are running on patience fumes.

Now whenever I have an appointment at a doctor, hair stylist, or other place, I feel the minutes tick away as if a bomb taped to me was counting off the seconds before exploding!

I heard someone say the definition of "in the twinkling of an eye" is the time it takes when a traffic light turns green before the person behind you honks their horn for you to hurry up and go already. Yes, we have a shortage of patience these days.

What do you do during those times when you are left waiting because of something out of your control?

What about this . . . how many times have we told God we will talk with him when we get a spare moment? Yet, how many extra minutes do we have in our day, when waiting on someone, that we could spend chatting with God? Are we redeeming the time or frittering it away? God can use those waiting rooms to help us feel closer to him. To do that, we need to draw near to him. He hasn't budged—we've just drifted away in our distractions of to-do lists and bad attitudes and other issues. They clutter our minds and hearts.

> *Let us go right into the presence of God with sincere hearts fully trusting him. For our guilty consciences have been sprinkled with Christ's blood to make us clean, and our bodies have been washed with pure water.*
> (Hebrews 10:22)

We need to kick the mental clutter to the curb, or at least put blinders on to it. (I'm good at having blinders when it comes to real clutter in my home.) Then we can zero in on what really matters. Time with God.

During the PAUSE

Pray

Father, I'm not coping very well with this pause. Help me find something special right now to focus on rather than getting discouraged by the delay. Guard me from discouragement as I wait.

Adjust

I will trade my impatience for a new coping skill to help reframe my outlook.

Undertake

I will start a new journal (on the computer, online, or handwritten) to vent my frustrations.

Seek

I will look for something happening that I would miss if I weren't experiencing this delay.

Evaluate

I will examine how serious my impatience is so I can deal with it before it turns to bitterness.

QUOTE: "The greatest lesson I have learned in the holding patterns of life is to wait on the Lord. Your Pilot knows the destination and the exact time to bring you into it. Remember that God can do more in an instant than we can in a lifetime." –Dr. Scott Pauley[4]

ME in the RAW: I can barely trust the pilot, who I *can* see. How am I going to trust the control tower, which I *can't* see? I would rather take control of the plane and fly it myself, only I've never had a flying lesson!

ME in the SPIRIT: Lord, I trust you in this holding pattern. I know you can see the whole picture. I will wait for you to land me on this journey, to the destination of your choosing, in your desired timeline.

Chapter Four

NOT KNOWING IS NOT NO-ING

So often, when we feel clueless and we aren't getting answers, it feels as if God is telling us no. Then we tend to go down the dangerous spiral, wondering what we've done wrong to deserve this and what we need to do to receive God's yes. We assume we've done something on the no-no list and are being punished when in truth, the wait is designed to strengthen us for a new thing.

When a Parent Says No

It's not fair of me to mention terrible parenting skills since I haven't been blessed with children, but I think I can point out some techniques that are *so* wrong that I won't catch any flack for the criticism. Besides, they're too funny to be serious—almost. Top three "No-No" no-nos:

1.   **Count Parentula.** "Johnny! I'm counting to five, and then you're in big trouble if you don't quit kicking the back of my car seat. One. Two. Three. Four. Four and a fourth. Four and a half. Four and four/sixths. Four and three/

fourths. Four and seven/eights—Oh, look at that giraffe on the side of the road!"

2. **The cool parent.** "Kimmie, I said no. No means no! No, it doesn't mean yes. Yes, it means no. Wait. Now you've got me confused. Just go play while I figure it out." (Turns to mom friend on play date.) "I can't remember. Is yes the new no?"

3. **The forgetful parent.** "Wait until we get home. You're gonna get it. Wait 'til I tell your dad. You're in big trouble. When we get home, you're going directly to your room. When we get home" . . . "Hey, we're home! Do you want pizza tonight?"

> The wait is designed to strengthen us for a new thing.

I can't even pretend to imagine I know what it's like to have to discipline your precious offspring when they willfully misbehave. If it were me, I'd be thinking: "They are adorable, they entertain me with their silly antics, and they look just like me." But correction and discipline are necessary to give children direction to help them learn life skills that last a lifetime.

When I was a child, one of the worst sentences authority figures could say to me was, "You should be ashamed of yourself." I've lived my whole life hearing that condemnation of me. It's as if the accusation echoes in my head. There's a song by Tasha Layton called "Look What You've Done" that could have been written by me. Instead of receiving that condemnation for self, flip the script and think about all the amazing things God has done. I need to make sure I don't think God is the one scolding me. Especially when I'm in the middle of a waiting period, feeling like God is delaying my help. The Bible says, *So now there is no condemnation for those who belong to Christ Jesus* (Romans 8:1).

Often, we assume God treats his children just like parents treat their own here on earth. But that's simply not the case. Every time we don't get what we want, when we want it, it's not necessarily discipline from God. We aren't always being punished when we're in a holding pattern. God might not be saying, "No." He's simply saying, "Not now."

When Jesus Delayed

Mary and Martha knew all about delays. They sent for Jesus to come and heal their brother Lazarus, but by the time he showed up, their brother had already been stinking in the grave for four days. It wasn't merely that Jesus was delayed on the road due to rush hour or a traffic accident—he purposely waited a couple of days before starting his journey. He obviously had a reason for putting their request on hold. *

The disciples didn't get it when Jesus said Lazarus was asleep (dead) or understand why he waited to be with Mary and Martha. Jesus explained to the disciples that the delay was so they

> We may be stuck in the middle of a stinky mess, but up ahead is a miracle!

could see God at work. The outcome of waiting would be *"for the glory of God so that the Son of God will receive glory from this"* (John 11:4).

Can you imagine how Mary and Martha would have felt if they had known Jesus intentionally waited to come? It's possible they expected Jesus to drop everything to come to their aid. If we're honest, when we face a delay, we become disgruntled by God's holdups as well. We have unrealistic expectations. We think we can pray and have our wishes become God's commands. It doesn't work that way.

---

* John 11

When Jesus showed up at Mary and Martha's, look at their response. Mary, normally the one most demonstrative in worshiping Jesus, held back while Martha greeted him. But it wasn't a pleasant welcome. Martha said, *"Lord, if only you had been here, my brother would not have died. But even now I know that God will give you whatever you ask"* (John 11:21–22).

> God loves us too much to let us settle for mediocre.

I'm not sure what changed about Mary or what caused her initial hesitation in greeting Jesus, but once Jesus came to the house, she fell at his feet. She then said almost the same words as Martha when she finally spoke. *"Lord, if only you had been here, my brother would not have died"* (John 11:32). I wonder if she flashed back to when she fell at his feet earlier?[*]

What happened next? Mary, Martha, and the entourage who mourned with them witnessed the miracle. Then maybe they understood the purpose of the delay a little better. They watched Jesus weep and call Lazarus out of the grave, defeating death. They saw Jesus in an even greater display of strength.

If Jesus had made the trip when the sisters first requested, they might have seen a sick Lazarus healed, but due to what seemed like a delay, they witnessed a full-fledged resurrection! What appeared to be a late entrance was a perfectly on-time arrival.

We might miss the miracle if we choose to stay stuck in our disappointment and despair. And when we wallow in gloom, we blame our Lifesaver prematurely—before his time to rescue us.

Our delays might feel like the four days between the death of Lazarus and his return to life. During that time, he was bound by his death clothes, decaying—a stinky mess of cells disassembling, and trapped in a dark place.

Can you relate? What does your "in-between" look like? We

---

[*] Luke 10:39

may be stuck in the middle of a stinky mess, but up ahead is a miracle. Sometimes between the *wait* and the *yes*, we need to fall at Jesus's feet and be caught up in total adoration of the Savior.

When God delays in answering our prayers, it's not always a *no* response. And it's not because he's dropped us from his favorite people list. But it's easy for us to blame him when we don't get the answer we expected in the timeframe we expected it.

Maybe our request is too small for God—it certainly isn't too big. Maybe if he waits, he will get *big* glory and see a *big* expansion of the kingdom. If we knew the wait would result in magnifying God and his work, would we let go of our expectations and pick up more patience? The issue isn't that God *can't* help us or that he *won't* help us—it's that we want to give up too soon. The problem isn't that God doesn't love us enough to respond in a timely manner to our request—it's that he loves us too much to let us settle for mediocre.

Bucking against God

I felt like a cowgirl. I sat proudly on the saddle. Held on to the reins with just one hand and raised one above my head as I'd seen those rodeo girls do. I was only nine. But the horse began to buck. It was a rocky ride. I had lost control. And did I tell you that this was an old-fashioned bouncy toy horse? The springs boinged out of control, and before I knew it, I was bucked off the horse.

> I will practice not assuming a delay means "no." It merely means wait.

OUCH! It hurt. My pride hurt more. I was the oldest cousin, and I was supposed to look as if I had everything under control. Right. I couldn't even fool myself, let alone others. I didn't like it when I got knocked off that horsey.

Now that I'm a grown woman (*full* grown at that!), I realize I'm still bucking. I buck against what I know is best. I buck against others. And worst of all, occasionally I buck against God. Especially when he's not operating on my timetable and not answering my questions.

Have more questions than answers? Maybe God will let you in on the secret. But frequently, the best growth is in the not knowing. And sometimes, because Jesus loves us, he does *nothing*. Why is that? So he can get *more* glory.

During the PAUSE

Pray

Father, help me tell the difference between not knowing the outcome and your no. I want to learn to be okay with waiting. Strengthen me for what you are preparing in my future.

Adjust

I will practice not assuming a delay means no. It merely means wait. I will throw out any negative thought that hinders me from receiving God's strength during this season of my life.

Undertake

I will add in more physical activity to my routine. While waiting for the *new thing* to arrive, I'll work on physical strengthening and endurance. It will help compensate for my still-weak areas.

Seek

I will look for Bible verses that assure me I'm secure in Christ and no longer face condemnation.

Evaluate

I will scrutinize if there's something about my circumstance that makes me feel as though God isn't being fair with me. How do I determine what I think I deserve? Once I identify these aspects, I'll yield my thoughts to God.

> **QUOTE:** "The secret in all our life experiences is to be at peace and accept God's timing." –AnnMarie Anderson[5]
>
> **ME in the RAW:** But I don't want to accept his timing—I want it *now!*
>
> **ME in the SPIRIT:** God's "wait" is merely my cue that he's working things out. The prettiest flowers take a while to grow. Just when I think they're not going to bloom, they blossom in all their glory!

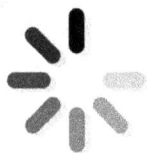

Chapter Five

THE ELUSIVE ANSWER

G oing through this waiting period wouldn't seem so long if we
could just have a few answers along the way—like a glimmer
of light at the end of the dark tunnel. How can we find wisdom
and discernment while we're going through a pause? Sometimes
we need to ask different questions—to find the answers waiting to
be discovered. Other times, part of the wait is not having answers
yet still trusting. Faith is in the not knowing.

Why the Delay?

If God plans to answer my prayer request with yes, why does he
allow or cause a delay and make me wait? In Acts 1:7, Jesus tells the
disciples, *"The Father alone has the authority to set those dates and
times, and they are not for you to know."* While that statement was
for a specific question from the disciples, I don't think it is far off
for our questions regarding our wait. We don't need to bother our
minds by wondering when the right timing will be. Our reasoning
won't work to try to figure out God anyway. Isaiah 55:8 says, *"My
thoughts are nothing like your thoughts,"* says the Lord. *"And my ways
are far beyond anything you could imagine."*

We can be sure of one thing, though. We can know that God has our best interests in mind when he allows the timing and direction of our situations. Ecclesiastes 3:11 says, *Yet God has made everything beautiful for its own time. He has planted eternity in the human heart, but even so, people cannot see the whole scope of God's work from beginning to end.*

Faith is in the not knowing.

Seeking wisdom? It's in the "not-knowing" that we learn the most. Then we trust in someone other than ourselves. Waiting for the elusive answer reminds me of the television remote. The remote setting during this delay? It seems as if God is on mute, and I am on pause. Wouldn't it be great if hearing from God was as simple as unmuting the remote? Getting out of this delay would be as simple as unpausing my life!

> *Enthusiasm without knowledge is no good; haste makes mistakes.*
>
> (Proverbs 19:2)

We make matters worse when we rush ahead of God and try to fix our own problems. We think the inaction of our pause means action is required on our part, and we act hastily. (Similar to the person who fills every silent pause of conversation with chatter because she can't stand the quiet.) What happens when we are in a hurry, but it seems like God isn't? (Don't forget God isn't on our timeline—in fact, time is irrelevant to him. A day is as a thousand years to God and vice versa.) Has it ever worked to try to get God to hurry up? It just helps us grow more impatient looking for that hard-to-pinpoint answer or solution.

It might start with good intentions. You get a dream from God, a passion that becomes a goal when you decide to say yes to it. But then the delays start to come, just like orange barrels in construction zones on our highway toward the destination. We decide to take a detour that isn't on the route—take things into our own hands. Just like Abraham (Abram) and Sarah (Sarai) when she couldn't get pregnant. Rather than wait for God's timing in delivering Abraham a son, Abraham took the servant Hagar to bed to create a legacy.* But it wasn't God's plan. And anything that isn't in God's plan turns into problems. Thankfully, God can take problems and turn them into something good.

We need to wait to get the answer that truly comes from God.

Have you ever waited so long that you started second-guessing yourself—doubting that you really heard from God to begin with? *If God led me to set these goals, why did he allow them to get put on hold? Maybe he doesn't really want me to do these things after all. Maybe I just imagined it all. Maybe it was simply wishful thinking. God doesn't want to use me!* See the dangerous leap we make when we start to doubt?

> The delay is part of the growth process to ensure I'm ready—ripe for the purpose at hand.

People often live mediocre lives because they've settled for less than what God had in mind. They make a compromise to get out of the wait prematurely. There's no get-out-of-jail-free card. All we can do is choose to not look at our pause as though it's jail.

> *So let's not get tired of doing what is good. At just the right time we will reap a harvest of blessing if we don't give up.*
>
> (Galatians 6:9)

The harvest is all about good timing. Reaping never comes immediately following planting—there is always a delay. This is the season God is at work to mature the crop. In my life, that is the time he is at work developing the fruit of the Spirit. The delay isn't a negative scenario. It's part of the growth process to ensure I'm ready—ripe for the purpose at hand.

---

* Genesis 16

47

> God is forever present with us.
> Having him with us is more important
> than having—well, anything!

*And he told them a parable to the effect that they ought
always to pray and not lose heart.*

(Luke 18:1 ESV)

What happens if we pray on, even when the trials come or we
enter a waiting room in our lives? What if consistent prayer leads
to the second part of the verse—the ability to not be disheartened?
Or perhaps prayer plus encouragement leads to something more.

Questions We Tend to Ask the Lord

- How long will my life be on hold?
- What am I supposed to learn so I can get out of this hold-
  ing pattern?
- What did I do wrong that caused this pause?
- Why do I have to wait for my desired outcome when oth-
  ers who are less godly are enjoying *my* reward?

Questions We Need to Ask the Lord

- Will you help me sense your presence more clearly as I wait?
- What can I learn about you while I wait?
- What can I learn about myself while I wait?
- How can I still be active in your work while I wait?
- How can I reflect your grace while I wait?

Does God Hear?

Do you feel God is ignoring your prayers as you pour out your
heart to him? When you have a delay in seeing your prayers answered, does it feel as if God isn't listening to you? Or as if he can't

hear. But since when do we use the word *can't* when describing God's abilities? Of course, he hears. Delays don't indicate God is ignoring us, but it might indicate he is using this time to restore us (or to restore someone else learning from our pause).

Sometimes, we need the delay for God to prepare us

> I will look for God at work and get involved in that activity while waiting for my answer.

for the answer he is customizing for his purpose to come true in our lives. Our job when we sense silence on the other end of our prayers is simple. Wait. And in the wait, we trust. And in the trust, we grow patience. And when patience has grown up, it becomes endurance. Then we're ready to run the faith marathon designed with us in mind.

Isn't it curious that the very thing that causes us to feel impatient is an example of God's patience? We think he's being quiet, or even absent from our lives because of our situation. The opposite is true—he is forever present with us. Having God with us is more important than having—well, anything!

During the PAUSE

Pray

Father, I sure wish I could see some light to know this dark tunnel is about to end. Instead, I can't see my hand, let alone see your hand. Help me have faith when I don't have answers.

Adjust

I will change my expectation of getting fast answers to this lull and choose to hold on instead.

Undertake

I will learn to see waiting as an important step in the process, not one to rush.

Seek

I will look for God at work and get involved in that activity while waiting for my answer.

Evaluate

I will ponder how I can make this prolonged delay into an opportunity to serve God differently.

QUOTE: "I do know that waiting on God requires the willingness to bear uncertainty, to carry within oneself the unanswered question, lifting the heart to God about it whenever it intrudes upon one's thoughts." –Elisabeth Elliot[6]

ME in the RAW: How can I find the open door if I don't have the answer key to find my way? Details! I need details!

ME in the SPIRIT: May the Father help me to be okay with not knowing the answers I seek and realize life is more than this trivial pursuit.

Chapter Six

THE PRESENT OF HIS PRESENCE

God gives us the one thing we need while we wait to get un-stuck. He endows us with his presence. This is as vital as breathing—to be aware of God's presence right here with us. And his presence is enough. Everything else we could wish for has the potential to let us down, but God's presence is a constant we can depend on. We draw strength and comfort from him, enough to counter the agony of the wait.

While we're waiting to get out of a holding pattern, we think we're waiting for God to show up. But he's already here with us, loving us, hurting because we hurt. Instead, we tend to believe the lies from the Enemy. He taunts us and deceives us with words similar to these:

- God doesn't love you, or he wouldn't make you suffer.
- God doesn't want you to be happy.
- God isn't listening to your prayers.
- God loves someone else more and blesses them more.
- God is withholding blessing from you because you don't have enough faith.
- God is punishing you for unconfessed sin in your life.

In the Meantime

We don't like waiting because we don't know what to do in the meantime. Meantime isn't really mean. But it feels like the bully of time, ticking away the seconds, minutes, hours, days, weeks, months, and years as we wait to get out of the holding pattern.

> We draw strength and comfort from God, enough to counter the agony of the wait.

So how do we reverse that perspective? We can't look at it as being mean (a bully). But that it *means* something. The wait means something. We don't merely get answers at the end of our wait—we get something right now, before we know anything or have any direction or make one step toward what seems like progress. We get shaped, refined, refreshed, refueled—this wait means something. Just like a musical rest means something in a piece of music.

Just like the *selah* meant something to the psalmist.[7]

Meantime isn't mean to me. It means something to me.

Pastor Rick Ezell preached, "Waiting is not just something we have to do while we get what we want. Waiting is the process of becoming what God wants us to be. What God does in us while we wait is as important as what it is we are waiting for . . . Waiting is the confident, disciplined, expectant, active, and sometimes painful clinging to God."[8]

> *For God has not given us a spirit of fear and timidity,*
> *but of power, love, and self-discipline.*
>
> (2 Timothy 1:7)

Not Alone in the Wait

As Jesus prepared the disciples for his departure, he instructed them to wait for his return. And he said he was sending the Comforter. That shows me there are two things we can be sure of in this world.

THE PRESENT OF HIS PRESENCE

1. **We're supposed to wait.** Not just for his return but for anything he chooses to delay. (Which is really right on time by his plan.)

2. **Jesus didn't intend for us to feel alone in our wait.** In the meantime, the Spirit would be with us. This shows me God's presence is the most important aspect for our focus during any time we feel on hold. He comforts us, which proves it's human to feel uncomfortable (downright miserable!) during the wait and long for comfort. We wouldn't need a Comforter if we could handle it on our own, would we?

In Luke 11:13, Jesus said, *"If you, then, being evil [that is, sinful by nature], know how to give good gifts to your children, how much more will your heavenly Father give the Holy Spirit to those who ask and continue to ask Him!"* (AMP).

I find it interesting that Luke, a doctor by trade, mentioned Jesus's quote about our heavenly Father giving us the Holy Spirit as a gift. (In Matthew, the same passage just says gifts, but Luke expounded on it.) There is no gift like the Holy Spirit living in us. It makes all the other things we pray for (which is what that part of the Sermon on the Mount discusses) worth the wait. We need the Spirit to keep us sane while we're in a holding pattern.

> The wait means something. We get shaped, refined, refreshed, refueled—this wait means something.

Waiting as a Gift

James 1:2–4 in the New Living Translation says, *Dear brothers and sisters, when troubles of any kind come your way, consider it an opportunity for great joy. For you know that when your faith is tested, your endurance has a chance to grow.*

53

The Message paraphrase words that passage this way:

> *Consider it a sheer gift, friends, when tests and challenges come at you from all sides. You know that under pressure, your faith-life is forced into the open and shows its true colors. So don't try to get out of anything prematurely. Let it do its work so you become mature and well-developed, not deficient in any way.*

When we see waiting as a gift, we can have joy in the wait. (Other translations say, *Count it all joy.*) We need endurance to deal with life stuff, and waiting is the proving ground for endurance and patience.

Just as the disciples waited for the Lord's return, our wait requires that we trust in the Lord. Not just any ol' trust, but *patient* trust. That's easier said than done, isn't it? Patience takes growth, and when we grow more patience, we grow godliness. When we trust in God, we give him the benefit of the doubt that he knows what he's doing. Of course, he does—he's God! But sometimes we forget that and want to rush things, fix things, move on. Trust slows down the whirling desire to *do* something and allows us to wait.

> Trust slows down the whirling desire to *do* something and allows us to wait.

Interesting for us who have come after Jesus's first disciples. We who have been given the presence of the Holy Spirit dwelling inside us. His Spirit brings gifts, according to Galatians 5:22–23. One of those gifts is patience. We need it, don't we? *But the Holy Spirit produces this kind of fruit in our lives: love, joy, peace, patience, kindness, goodness, faithfulness, gentleness, and self-control. There is no law against these things!* And we need these other attributes of being Spirit-filled too!

When we wait and don't take matters into our own hands, we are saying we know God is in control, and we follow his lead.

It's hard to let go of the reins, but the truth is, we don't hold them anyway—we just like to *think* we do.

> [2] *May God give you more and more grace and peace as you grow in your knowledge of God and Jesus our Lord.*
>
> [3] *By his divine power, God has given us everything we need for living a godly life. We have received all of this by coming to know him, the one who called us to himself by means of his marvelous glory and excellence.*
>
> [4] *And because of his glory and excellence, he has given us great and precious promises. These are the promises that enable you to share his divine nature and escape the world's corruption caused by human desires.*
>
> [5] *In view of all this, make every effort to respond to God's promises. Supplement your faith with a generous provision of moral excellence, and moral excellence with knowledge,*
>
> [6] *and knowledge with self-control, and self-control with patient endurance, and patient endurance with godliness,*
>
> [7] *and godliness with brotherly affection, and brotherly affection with love for everyone.*
>
> [8] *The more you grow like this, the more productive and useful you will be in your knowledge of our Lord Jesus Christ.*
>
> (2 Peter 1:2–8)

Patience is included in the building blocks of the faith found in the above passage. Notice what we are to build before patient endurance can be formed: self-control. Maybe we are having trouble enduring with patience because we have little self-control. And keep in mind, self-control in this context means the control that comes when we give the Spirit 100 percent control, and because of him, we are able to resist temptation and give ourselves boundaries.

Definitions of patient

> 1: bearing pains or trials calmly or without complaint
> 2: manifesting forbearance under provocation or strain
> 3: not hasty or impetuous
> 4: steadfast despite opposition, difficulty, or adversity
> 5a: able or willing to bear[9]

The Right Time

As we wait, we realize it often takes time for God to work out the intricate details of the end result. The holding pattern doesn't mean nothing is happening—it means God is at work while we trust his timing to be best. We don't rush a fine cheesecake as it bakes—pulling it too soon results in a jiggly, mushy mess. We have to wait for just the right time. And God is the only one who knows what that timing is.

> I will look at this wait as having meaning to me, not as being mean to me.

Trusting God is at the heart of waiting. And the only way to trust someone is to be near them. And when we're with them often, we start becoming like them. Soon, we are refreshed and strengthened so that at just the right time, we can move forward again.

> *But those who trust in the Lord will find new strength.*
> *They will soar high on wings like eagles. They will run*
> *and not grow weary. They will walk and not faint.*
> (Isaiah 40:31)

Waiting isn't only for the purpose of biding our time while God works out the details. It grows us. Strengthens us. Not merely because we checked another day off the calendar. No—growth happens as we focus on God's presence in our lives and enjoy his company.

Receive his comfort. Be challenged by his questions. Find consolation and exhortation in his Word. In the meantime, God's presence is enough.

During the PAUSE

Pray

Holy Spirit, thank you for living in me and inserting your patience into my impatient situation. Help me endure with gladness so that Papa God gets the glory—because of Jesus.

Adjust

I will look at this wait as having meaning to me, not as being mean to me.

Undertake

I will use this wait to draw closer to God. His presence is a present in the meantime.

Seek

I will look for opportunities to build more patient endurance rather than getting in a rush.

Evaluate

I will make sure I'm practicing the self-control of God-in-control since that builds patience.

QUOTE: "He makes us wait. He keeps us on purpose in the dark. He makes us walk when we want to run, sit still when we want to walk, for He has things to do in our souls that we are not interested in." –Elisabeth Elliot[10]

ME in the RAW: I don't like being made to do anything! And the dark? No, thank you. I'm designed for the light.

ME in the SPIRIT: May God do a work in my soul. I will slow down now so I can soar later.

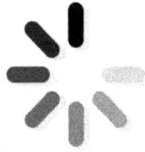

Chapter Seven

TEST OF TRUST

While we're waiting, enduring, and holding on, it feels a lot like a test. Sometimes it's not a trial to punish us for what we've done wrong, but a test to see what we'll do right. It's a test of trust. Will we lean on God or try to lean on our own abilities—or those of others? Often, we can discover who we're relying on when we check to see who we run to during life's challenges.

Failed the Test

When it came to schoolwork, I did pretty well with taking tests. And I didn't have test anxiety like some students. Most of the time, I was well prepared. Then there was the driver's test. Warning: uncomfortable confession ahead. I grew up around cars. My dad tinkered on vehicles in the garage, and I loved hanging out with him there. As long as I didn't talk, Dad didn't mind. By the time I was in high school, I knew all the basics about automobiles. Carburetors. Spark plugs. Oil filters. Head gaskets. Then when I started going out with Russ, we considered it a good date if we went to the junkyards or drooled over car magazines together.

So, cars were obviously not the problem. But something was—

because I was not a good driver. I made others nervous. My parents decided to wait and let the Driver's Ed teacher train me. Everyone else in class already knew how to drive.

One of the requirements to pass Driver's Ed was to drive across Champ Clark Bridge. The old bridge was a very narrow five-span truss bridge crossing the Mississippi River. On my day to drive, we had a fresh batch of ice and snow. Not good driving conditions. But the teacher believed we needed to know how to drive in inclement weather, so he took us out on the roads. That might have been fine for the others, experienced as they were. But not me.

> The experience we gain as we do life is what preps us for the next situation that arises.

I'll never forget Ricky Stephens lying on the back seat floor, eyes closed, as I attempted to cross the bridge. Was he being silly, or was he scared to death? I seem to remember him trembling, which I don't think was part of the prank. Somehow, I made it, and somehow, I passed Driver's Ed.

Because of that experience, I waited an entire year to take my driver's test. Then, right before my brother turned sixteen, I took the test. I didn't want him to surpass me. Getting a license was a rite of passage, and I would have been embarrassed if Wade got there before me. Despite all the horror stories everyone told me, and the fact that I botched up the parallel parking maneuver, I passed the very first time. No one could believe it—not even me!

After graduating to adulthood, I figured there would be no more tests. No one told me about taking medical tests when symptoms surface. How does a patient go about prepping for these tests? I'm not talking about that prep that requires drinking icky fluids and then . . . ahem . . . leaking icky fluids. I'm referring to studying for the test so that you pass. How can a patient get good grades? I wish I knew because for the past thirty-plus years, I seem to have failed the tests. There's no practice test for lab work, I suppose.

And just as there is no study aid to pass medical testing, there's no way to study for tests in life. Or is there? I'm thinking the act of living *is* the preparation for the test. The experience we gain as we do life is what preps us for the next situation that arises.

Are there other ways we can prep for the test?

Trust Fall or Trust Fail?

There is a team-building exercise called the trust fall. The team stands behind the individual taking the test. He must fall backward, blindly and confidently, hoping the others catch him. This requires great trust. To succeed, it only takes believing they will do what they say they will and then acting on that trust. But if there is no faith, trust fails, and the individual chickens out. He can't put control into the hands of others. He walks away. A trust fail.

> I can continue to have faith when I put my trust in the One who makes all the difference.

God tested the Israelites during their forty-year wilderness adventure to see how they would respond under pressure. It also tested their loyalty and obedience to him. Would they follow him at all costs or compromise to pick the easier way of life? It was a test of trust. Deuteronomy 8:2 says, "*Remember how the Lord your God led you through the wilderness for these forty years, humbling you and testing you to prove your character, and to find out whether or not you would obey his commands.*"

The test of trust is to see if we really have faith that God can do it. What messes up our idyllic faith is that we have lived a life of sight, witnessing so many times when things went wrong. So then comes the pause, the holding pattern, the waiting room time when we attempt to balance faith and sight.

Living by Sight or by Faith?

Faith knows God *can* do it. Sight knows people's mistakes have interrupted that perfect plan. I don't really struggle with my faith that God can do whatever I hope to see accomplished. I know he can do it. He is able. But I don't have confidence in other people.

> We make mistakes and God makes miracles.

Over time, I've experienced too much human error for me to put my complete trust in them.

This is especially true in my experience with the medical profession. I have lived by sight, having so many things go wrong for so long that my view from medical experience hinders me from having trust in them. I work to find the balance between faith and sight. I believe God can intervene whenever he deems best. Why does he do this occasionally but not always? I'm not sure. But I know when he does come to my rescue, he gets big glory. And perhaps the times when I'm left in the waiting rooms (literally and figuratively), it is because there is more to be accomplished without a miraculous intervention.

Even the famous academic medical centers that are known for their focus on integrated health care, education, and research dropped the ball on my case. All my negative experiences have clouded my view—my perspective. However, I can trust God to make it okay no matter *what* happens—whether he steps in to fix what is broken or whether he wants me to go through a less-than-optimal situation.

Similar to how steroid-induced cataracts blur my vision so much it's like looking through frosted glass, my belief is out of focus unless I focus on the One who clears my vision. I can continue to have faith when I put my trust in the One who makes all the difference.

I choose to lean into God even when mistakes happen and know that loving him and receiving his love is enough. He makes it okay no matter what happens. It reminds me of the anonymous quote that says, "Today's test is tomorrow's testimony." What is a Christ follower's testimony? It is their life story of loving God and living for him as he interacts in their lives. It comes with seeing God at work in and through their one-of-a-kind experiences with trials and victories.

Jeremiah endured an intense test of trust as he served the Lord and spoke the Word of God despite unbearable opposition. He had nearly lost hope. *I cry out, "My splendor is gone! Everything I had hoped for from the Lord is lost!"* (Lamentations 3:18). We see that he found himself in his own waiting room. *So it is good to wait quietly for salvation from the Lord.* (Lamentations 3:26). When he hit rock bottom, he yielded to God and experienced renewed hope.

Look at what Jeremiah faced as he waited for God to work:

- Weariness (Lamentations 3:1–5)
- Affliction (Lamentations 3:1)
- Chastisement (Lamentations 3:1)
- Dark despair (Lamentations 3:2)
- Persistent pain (Lamentations 3:3–4)
- Confinement (Lamentations 3:6–7)
- Obstructed path to God (Lamentations 3:8–9)
- Desolation (Lamentations 3:10–13)
- Bullied and rejected (Lamentations 3:14–16)
- Chaos instead of peace (Lamentations 3:17–19)
- Hopelessness (Lamentations 3:18–19)
- Bitterness (Lamentations 3:19)
- Misery (Lamentations 3:20)

Do you recognize any of your own waiting room experiences in the above list?

Jeremiah's turning point becomes our to-do list:

- Hit rock bottom (Lamentations 3:53–55)
- Pray from the bottom of the pit (Lamentations 3:55)

- Embrace humility (Lamentations 3:20–21)
- Dare to hope again (Lamentations 3:21)
- Call on the Lord (Lamentations 3:55–57)
- Recall the Lord's goodness (Lamentations 3:25)
- Depend on God (Lamentations 3:25–26)
- Wait patiently for God (Lamentations 3:25–26)
- Seek God (Lamentations 3:25–26)
- Sit alone and keep silent (Lamentations 3:28–29)
- Instead of complaining, wait for hope to show up. (Lamentations 3:28–29)
- Endure correction (Lamentations 3:30–33)
- Examine your heart, your words, your actions, your attitudes (Lamentations 3:37–42)
- Turn toward God's plan (Lamentations 3:40)
- Receive God's instruction to hope rather than fear (Lamentations 3:57–58)

The source of Jeremiah's hope can be ours too. Lamentations 3:22–24 says: *The faithful love of the Lord never ends! His mercies never cease. Great is his faithfulness; his mercies begin afresh each morning. I say to myself, "The Lord is my inheritance; therefore, I will hope in him!"*

Ask yourself:

- What does it mean to me that God's love and mercies never end?
- How great is his faithfulness to me?
- What new mercy do I receive each morning?
- How special is it for the Lord to be my inheritance?
- Is this enough reason for me to hang my hope on him?

During the PAUSE

Pray

Lord, I want to believe. Help me when I don't believe because of all the messes around me. We make mistakes, and you make miracles. Help me hold on to that during this current test of trust.

Adjust

I will quit focusing on what is going wrong and, instead, look at the God who makes things right.

Undertake

I will find one thing I can act on now while I wait. Often when I'm in a test of trust, I get so frustrated that I feel paralyzed. This wait doesn't have to stall me out.

Seek

I will look for someone else to bless while I wait. Even a cup of cold water offered in Jesus's name can make a difference in someone else's life.*

Evaluate

I will look for any issue causing me to have difficulty trusting God. I will change my perspective and trust him before my circumstances change.

---

* Matthew 10:42

QUOTE: "In trust, you do not look for security in other things; you look to God to hold you securely in difficult circumstances." –Brittany Yesudasan[11]

ME in the RAW: I've been burned by trust before. How can I know God's got me?

ME in the SPIRIT: Because God is trustworthy, I will trust him with my whole heart—even in this difficult circumstance.

Chapter Eight

STRIPPED AWAY

To get to an apple's core, the outer skin and the inner flesh must be cut away until all that remains is the core that houses the apple's seeds. The heart. When our lives are on hold, we often feel like everything else is stripped away. We lose what matters to us. Layer by layer, it disappears until all we have left is God. This is the final test of trust.

How do you trust God when you've lost so much and have little to hold on to except hope in him? Is that enough to sustain you as you wait out whatever is next?

What Have You Lost?

None of us lives very long before experiencing the pain of losing something or someone dear to us. Belongings. Security. Loved ones. Status. Finances. Employment. We don't mean to, but often we have lingering remnants of pain despite experiencing the victory of trusting God through the suffering of loss. This is why it can be helpful for us to inventory our losses, putting them on paper or the computer screen to give them the weight and importance they deserve.

This past week I've been evaluating my personal losses. I'm choosing to do the hard work of exploring my grief, my wounds, my wants.

I'll share my inventory list of recent losses to see if you can relate to some of these. Here are several things that hit at once to cause this awareness of a lonely sadness.

- **Loss of health.** I've been unhealthy all my adult life, but my condition has recently intensified. While I had adjusted to my former chronic status, this new status takes getting used to. I've been diagnosed with immunodeficiency and am self-infusing immune globulin treatment. At the same time, I've had two surgeries put on hold so we can learn how to prevent surgical infections. And I've been diagnosed with another rheumatological disease that requires intensive treatment once we address the immune issues.

- **Loss of friendships.** I've had a couple of friends decide to quit on our relationship at a time when I really needed them. I miss my time with them. And there is pain from not knowing how they are doing. I fondly remember some amazing friendship communities and have a burning desire to figure out how to have that in this new season of life.

- **Lack of intimacy.** Several friends receive my active listening and caregiving encouragement, but they don't reciprocate. They don't know what matters to my heart because they haven't invested in asking me.

- **Loss of church family.** Due to moving during the pandemic to a new area, we have had to make the difficult decision to change churches. Our faith family was seventy minutes away. That was simply too far for active involvement. But how I mourn the loss of that church in my life. Being somewhere new will take getting used to. It's like starting over.

- **Change in personal ministry focus.** Different opportunities to be involved in public and private ministry have all vanished due to several causes. I'm at a loss for what my *next* might be.

- **Change in clientele.** Saying goodbye to some of my clients who are going in a different direction is super hard but even more difficult when several terminate our arrangement in the same year. I support their new focus, but I miss my time with them.

By acknowledging my emotions, I've been able to receive God's healing and his direction for how to move past it, becoming even better for having experienced it.

> I'm choosing to do the hard work of exploring my grief, my wounds, my wants.

Lamentations, Continued . . .

In chapter 7, we looked at how Jeremiah endured great suffering, hit rock bottom, and renewed his hope in the Lord. Let's examine Lamentations 3:14–26 to see what it's like to be stripped of all we think matters—until we realize God alone matters. The words in italics below are taken directly from the Bible, and the words following are my modern paraphrase or commentary.

Lamentations 3:14

My own people laugh at me. All day long they sing their mocking songs. I feel like Rudolph the Red-Nosed Reindeer, and the bullies don't let me play in any of their reindeer games!

Lamentations 3:15

He has filled me with bitterness and given me a bitter cup of sorrow to drink. In my distorted perceptions, I feel everyone else is drinking chai tea, and I've been given castor oil to glug.

69

Lamentations 3:16

He has made me chew on gravel. He has rolled me in the dust. I have Sjogren's syndrome induced dry mouth, so I can relate to the torment of this sensation.

> I am determined to risk hoping for a better tomorrow by reminding myself of how great God is.

Lamentations 3:17

Peace has been stripped away, and I have forgotten what prosperity is. I've been stripped of everything that makes for peace, so much so that there are times I can't even remember what it feels like to be blessed.

Lamentations 3:18

I cry out, "My splendor is gone! Everything I had hoped for from the Lord is lost!" Everything that made me *me* has disappeared. All the prior answered prayers seem like shadows now. Why should I continue to hope in a God who allowed this to happen?

Lamentations 3:19

The thought of my suffering and homelessness is bitter beyond words. I'm ashamed to admit it, but all that I've gone through is making me so bitter that I can no longer talk about it, let alone pray to God about it. I can't even anchor my heart to a place called *home.* There's nothing left. It's all gone. Stripped away.

Lamentations 3:20

I will never forget this awful time, as I grieve over my loss. What I've lost is so great, there's no way I'll get over it. I mourn it as much as I grieve the loss of a loved one. What more do I have to lose?

Lamentations 3:21

Yet I still dare to hope when I remember this. Even though I've hit rock bottom, I am determined to risk hoping for a better tomorrow by reminding myself of how great God is.

Lamentations 3:22
The faithful love of the Lord never ends! His mercies never cease. God's enduring love and mercy are enough for me to hope in when all else is stripped away. It's everything I need to build up my confident faith again.

Lamentations 3:23
Great is his faithfulness; his mercies begin afresh each morning. God's faithfulness is immense. How can I not hope in him? His mercies aren't only past tense—they refresh daily.

Lamentations 3:24
I say to myself, "The Lord is my inheritance; therefore, I will hope in him!" I'm determined to make sure my soul-talk matches up to God's truths and not this world's lies. I remind myself that inheriting what I gain in God is sufficient to fuel my hope.

> I will seek God as my remnant of hope when all seems lost.

Lamentations 3:25
The Lord is good to those who depend on him, to those who search for him. As I depend on God and continue to seek him even when the way is dark, I will receive his blessings on my life. I can trust him even when I can't trust myself (and definitely when I can't trust others).

Lamentations 3:26
So it is good to wait quietly for salvation from the Lord. Do I need to remind myself why it is good to wait on the Lord? Okay, I'll say it again. The Lord will rescue me. Trusting in that, I have everything I need to wait quietly—knowing he is God (and I am not).

When we find ourselves feeling down and out, what a comfort to know we are not alone in our struggles. Even Jeremiah felt consumed by defeating thoughts and rehearsed soul-talk.

During the PAUSE

Pray

Oh God. I don't like it when everything that makes me comfortable is stripped away. It's bad enough for others to see my flaws but worse yet knowing you see them. I confess to you my struggles—the ones you already know. And I trust you for the outcome.

Adjust

I will learn to trust God rather than trusting in what makes me feel comfortable.

Undertake

I will be willing to reveal the real me. Transparency will be my new stripped-down reality.

Seek

I will seek God as my remnant of hope when all seems lost.

Evaluate

I will examine my comfort zone and make sure it's really a faith zone—relying on God rather than myself.

QUOTE: "Each of us, no matter what state we're in is precious in the eyes of God. Each of us has a unique purpose. Each of us has value. And sometimes it takes all being stripped away for us to see our true identity in Him." –Joanna Smith[12]

ME in the RAW: But why can't I have God, my identity, *and* all the things that have been stripped away?

ME in the SPIRIT: As I let God define me, I realize my identity in him alone is more significant than the sum of all I've lost.

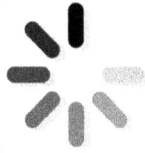

Chapter Nine

YIELDING AT THE STOP SIGN

W̲hat's more difficult—to yield or to stop? Either way, it slows us down from getting to our destination. Even worse is to have to yield at a stop sign, allowing the car to our right at a four-way stop to go before us. And in life, when we feel a lull, it's hard to slow down even more via yielding—submitting. To others, to God, to God's plan. Yielding is counter-intuitive in seeing results. When we let go of our natural bent to go-go-go, we see God-God-God.

Stopped in Traffic

Look at that gal talking with her hands. Inquisitive Kathy was at work again, noticing people living life out loud. *Wait a minute. She's not in a discussion. She's doing hand motions. Maybe she's using sign language.*

All the time I observed the girl in the car next to me at the stop sign, I was humming along with the radio. It was playing the praise song, "Lord I Lift Your Name on High." My thoughts drifted (as they are prone to do) to a previous youth service, remembering the touching motions that went with the song.

75

Then it dawned on me. I glanced over to the car next to me again and realized the driver was singing the same song I was singing, and she was also doing the motions—modified for driving. How inspiring to think that we were two women of many in that metropolitan area, tuned in to the same Christian radio station, singing the same song in our cars along a busy mall road. What is the likelihood of that happening? I don't know the odds, but I do know that others probably thought *we* were odd!

> When we let go of our natural bent to go-go-go, we see God-God-God.

I'm guessing God was blessed by our impromptu worship. We weren't meeting in a church building, but we were together in our focus on God in the middle of our busy days. He wasn't merely relegated to Sundays but also invited into our daily lives.

What other ways can we take a moment to yield to God while waiting for the green light? It's a good time to pray, as long as we don't close our eyes. I know someone who looks at flashcards to memorize Bible verses while he's driving, but I don't recommend it when the car is in motion, at least. Let's keep our eyes on the road while our hearts and minds visit with God. Even rush hour won't seem so dreadful when we realize we have company on the road.

We are so blessed to be able to praise God whenever we want, wherever we are. What would happen if we took our literal traffic slowdowns to slow down our thoughts and focus on God in that moment? It would put some calm in our chaos, some quietness in our noise, and maybe even give us some answers in our dilemmas.

Yielding at the Stop Sign

I have had so many times of waiting during my thirty-plus years of fighting chronic diseases and acute setbacks. One time I was hospitalized with a serious lung infection that mystified the doctors and caused sepsis (deadly multi-organ infection and inflammation). I was hospitalized for ten days, under home health care for a couple more months, and also sent to Mayo Clinic. The infection caused such a decline in my overall health, it took a lot to rebound. And at the same time, I had a rush order from a publisher to write a book, plus client work and ministry obligations. My health betrayed me, and I had to slow down despite my plans. As the saying goes, "Ain't nobody got time for that!"

What do you do when you have a forced timeout? I could have pouted like a child being disciplined. I knew that was the wrong response. So, I prayed and sought God's presence. There were too many outside-of-normal situations going on to be coincidental. I had peace that God planned to use my circumstances for a better good. It gave me what I needed to stay strong and wait while I watched God at work. I asked God to show me if I had allowed anything to get in the way of our relationship. Was something creating a barrier that needed to be removed before I received his answers to my prayers? God spoke peace over me. I knew for certain that the trial wasn't about me.

> Yielding puts some calm in our chaos, some quietness in our noise, and maybe even gives us some answers in our dilemmas.

Now, I know in life, it's *never* about me—it's about him. But in this case, the suffering wasn't to teach me a lesson or to get me to grow (although I did grow because suffering always creates an environment ripe for growth opportunities). But God impressed on my heart that this ongoing struggle with the medical professionals wasn't about my growth. No, instead, he would use it for the benefit of someone else (singular or plural). Knowing God could use it caused me to worship him even in my brokenness. And that is a beautiful thing.

(In hindsight, now ten years later, I have a friend who said she observed God at work in me at the time, and it taught her such a life-changing lesson that she still remembers it to this day.)

At the time, my hospitalist warned me to expect a long recovery. I wasn't surprised. I had a sense that I was close to death. I survived, but within ten days, I felt twenty years older. I couldn't even walk across the room without getting winded and lightheaded. I wasn't going to bounce back quickly. I was released to my primary care doctor once I came home. I'll never forget Russ wheeling me into the exam room, and I was masked due to a low immune system.

> Sometimes we need everything else to fall apart so we have the opportunity to learn how to not fall apart.

What came next was as severe a setback as the physical. My doctor informed me that he was leaving the practice, and that day was my final visit with him. No other doctor was filling his spot for a few months, and it was up to me to shop around for a new doctor. I could hardly keep my head up—how was I going to find a new doctor?

The first one I selected was an hour away. Russ drove me to the appointment. However, the doctor declined to take my case. I decided, rather than being discouraged, to be grateful he was humble enough to admit the case was too complex for him to take. But I still expected him to look over the list of recent symptoms my home health team wanted him to evaluate. Instead, his answer was just to give it time. It was disappointing that he deferred dealing with any of those urgent problems even though he knew it would take a while to be established somewhere else, just as it took a while to get in to see him.

The acute conditions really needed a doctor's attention ASAP. That's why it's called acute! It made no sense to me that he sent me on my way. They had set aside an hour for me as a new patient to meet with him, so I knew he had the time. He just didn't want to get into something he wasn't going to see through all the way. While I wasn't upset with him and could understand his thinking, it made me feel a bit "dropped."

At the same time, one of the keywords God had been speaking to my heart was the word *hold*. He was *holding* me, he wanted me to *hold* on, and he allowed several issues to be placed on *hold* for a reason. I reminded myself that the word *hold* was pretty much the opposite of the word *dropped*. The doctor may have dropped me, but God had me in his very capable, strong hands.

Sometimes we need everything else to fall apart so we have the opportunity to learn how to not fall apart. These times of yielding can certainly do that.

> *"If any of you wants to be my follower, you must give up your own way, take up your cross daily, and follow me. If you try to hang on to your life, you will lose it. But if you give up your life for my sake, you will save it."*

(Luke 9:23–24)

The Purpose of Pause

Waiting means yielding—allowing what happens (or doesn't happen) to be on God's timetable and not mine.

Every so often, we're not actually on hold. God is asking us to do something different than we want or expect so we can't do that other thing we want. It's either not right for us or not the right time. I've found God wants me to fully be in the moment when I experience some difficulties:

- Illness
- Being a family caregiver
- Poverty or financial struggles

We try to avoid painful experiences and say we want out of the holding pattern. But we aren't really in a holding pattern. We are exactly where God can use us.

We can hear God's voice in our hearts even in those times

when he doesn't reverse our painful struggles. This leads us to no longer resist yielding to God. It's a process.

"Here I am. Send me" becomes "Here I wait. Use me." Or, "Here I wait. Use this." Or simply "Here I wait. *Love* me."

Sometimes when God says, "Wait a little longer," we want to change it to "wait a little faster."

Waiting on God

Waiting on God means I seek his direction and won't act until he gives me peace about it. I wait on God to answer prayer. It's that time between when I first pray and when the answer comes.

When a waitress waits on us at a restaurant, our wish is her command. She is there to serve. When I wait on God, his wish is my command, and I'm here to serve him.

Waiting on God gives me more strength and hope because he is the one equipping me during the holding pattern. I don't have to rely on my own inferior strength when his ultimate power is available to me. During the wait, he recharges my batteries and provides rest.

> *You are my strength; I wait for you to rescue me, for you, O God, are my fortress.*

(Psalm 59:9)

During the PAUSE

Pray

Father, use my time of a forced slowdown to lean into you and yield to your work. Whether you use it for my growth or for the benefit of someone else, redeem this time for something of value.

Adjust

I will change my way of thinking regarding this yield. Submission is a beautiful thing.

Undertake

I will invest as much effort in slowing down as I usually do in being busy.

Seek

I will look for you in the yield, rather than looking for a solution.

Evaluate

I will determine if there's anything I'm doing that's getting in the way of your progress.

QUOTE: "Our heart is the scene of a divine operation more wonderful than creation. We can do as little towards the work as towards creating the world, except as God works in us to will and to do. God only asks of us to yield, to consent, and to wait upon Him, and He will do it all. Let us meditate and be still, until we see how good and right and blessed it is that God alone does all . . . Our soul will sink down in deep humility to say, *I have waited for Thy salvation, O Lord*. And the deep blessed background of all our praying and working will be *Truly my soul waiteth upon God*." –Andrew Murray[13]

ME in the RAW: How is "yielding" going to help me undo this holding pattern and get me moving forward again?

ME in the SPIRIT: I can't make my circumstances change—I can only change my heart and give it permission to worship God while I wait.

Chapter Ten

STAY QUIET AND BE STILL

No one likes to stay still when enduring trials. It feels better to keep busy, to be distracted, to create diversions. We often do the very opposite of what benefits us the most. It's too hard to stay still because that simply feels unproductive. But it's in the stillness where we meet with God. We rejuvenate as we rest in him. What we *learn* during the pause is as productive as what we *do* during the remainder of the journey.

Be Still!

Daddy didn't like my overactive hands and feet and . . . well . . . mouth. "Be still" was a pretty common phrase at our house. Sometimes Mom borrowed the expression. I guess I was a little too busy for their liking! When we were out on the fishing boat, Dad said I'd scare the fish off with all my talking. I learned how to be quiet. And Mom said I'd tip the boat over if I moved a muscle. So, I learned to be still. I didn't have to like it, though!

Every year we made a twelve-hour road trip to Oklahoma, where Mom grew up. That's a long time trapped in the car for even the best-behaved kids. My brother and I would get so bored sitting still that long—this was way before the days of electronic games, built-in video screens, and tablets. Dad and Mom took turns being annoyed with us. "Don't kick the seat, Kathy. Sit still. Don't bother your brother. Just look out the window." I guess the same disorder that attracted "Be still" in the boat followed me to the car.

> What we *learn* during the pause is as productive as what we *do* during the remainder of the journey.

Then there was the torture of the grocery store. (As a grown-up, I realize it was torture for Mom—not for me.) With two kids in tow, I'm not sure how Mom managed to concentrate on shopping to purchase enough groceries to feed us. I was attracted to the freebies in the popular caramel corn snack and breakfast cereals. My brother, Wade, liked looking at the sports cards with free gum (the most horrible-tasting brittle piece of gum on the planet earth, I think). We must have made for miserable shopping companions. But the torture for me was learning to be still. Even if we stayed in the car with Dad, we had to act like we weren't there so he could enjoy listening to the radio.

Those early disciplines taught me a lot. And I don't blame my folks one bit. I know I was high energy. The opposite of a sloth or a slug. But it wasn't only my parents who ordered, "Be still." The teacher expected us to be still on our braided nap rugs in kindergarten. I didn't want to take a nap! I wanted to play, to talk, to explore—even to learn. They could make me be still on the mat, but they couldn't make me sleep. My mind daydreamed. I learned how to play even when the rest of me had to act all nappy. If school nap time was designed to give my teacher a break, no one considered that she would have to remind me to *be still* so often.

I'll never forget the year my brave Sunday school teacher invited our class to stay for the worship service. It wasn't my routine to go to church as much as Sunday school, so proper church behavior was difficult for me. I was a good girl, but on the inside, I was miserable. You know why? Because of those two words the teacher spoke as a reminder when we walked into the sanctuary. "Be still."

It's obvious, that even from an early age I had a problem with being still.

> *Be still in the presence of the Lord, and wait patiently for him to act. Don't worry about evil people who prosper or fret about their wicked schemes.*
>
> (Psalm 37:7)

> *Let all that I am wait quietly before God, for my hope is in him.*
>
> (Psalm 62:5)

Waiting Rooms

Think about a waiting room in a doctor's office. That is where we prepare our hearts and minds for whatever the news might be when we walk into that exam room. Often the wait is *long*. It's difficult. The seats are uncomfortable. We see other people dealing with their own trials coming and going or waiting it out along with us.

We witness relieved patients coming out

We need each stage to equip us for what's next.

with the news, "benign." We see others come out with good news, "I'm expecting!" But some exit with shoulders stooped, heads lowered, perhaps to hide a tear. Six months to live. Our lives mirror that waiting room. What we do there prepares us for what is yet to come. I sense a change a-coming, and I'm glad for the waiting room to help me get ready for the news.

Life Hack for Being Still

> *Her sister, Mary, sat at the Lord's feet, listening to what he taught. But Martha was distracted by the*

85

big dinner she was preparing. She came to Jesus and said, "Lord, doesn't it seem unfair to you that my sister just sits here while I do all the work? Tell her to come and help me." But the Lord said to her, "My dear Martha, you are worried and upset over all these details! There is only one thing worth being concerned about. Mary has discovered it, and it will not be taken away from her."

(Luke 10:39–42)

What can we learn about being proactive by choosing to wait rather than trying to hurry, being overwhelmed with busyness? As we think about Mary's time at the feet of Jesus, we can pick up some life hacks for being still.

- Not sure what to do next? Instead of filling the time with busyness, slow down and sit at the feet of the Lord.

- What does it mean today when we're sitting at the Lord's feet? It's not a literal action because Jesus isn't in our home like he was with Mary. But he *is* here, isn't he? When I focus on God instead of the problems, that is my first step toward being still.

- Mary listened to what Jesus taught. How am I making sure to not just hear but listen to the Lord's teachings?

- In contrast, Martha was distracted by what needed to be done, worried and upset by all the details. And she felt life wasn't fair since her sister wasn't helping her. It's easy, when we're distracted, to put the blame on something or someone else. During the wait, there's no need to find fault or to compare our situations with the choices of others.

- If I'm going to allow myself to be concerned over something, what does this passage say is a worthy subject of my concern? Only one thing is worth it—sitting at the Lord's feet and listening to his teachings.

The Chrysalis Syndrome

Everyone has wonderful caterpillar-to-butterfly stories. I've written some into my books as well. But we don't talk much about the chrysalis stage.

If you're reading this book, you or someone you love is going through an "on hold" period. What if we looked at our holding pattern as a chrysalis? The time in between what was and what is to come. It's not a delay. It's not a wait. It's an on-purpose plan of pause. Nature experiences some sort of an in-between. Every winter, certain animals hibernate. Perennial plants often go dormant, only to bloom again in a new season.

There are many reasons why creation has these in-between stages, and there are many reasons why humans experience life on hold. Sometimes, it's to help us save our energy, like bears with a limited food supply that hibernate. Other times it's to transform us into something completely different, like a butterfly. But in all times, it's a situation that God can use for kingdom work.

The only way a chrysalis has bad news isn't because of the wait. It's because someone tries to rush the process and the butterfly never gets to fully develop. Or, if the butterfly emerges but is waiting for its wings to dry before flying—if someone rushes to adore it, the butterfly will die. It needs each stage to be strengthened and prepared for the next stage.

And we need each stage to equip us for what's next.

Rest Assured

Every year, I select a theme for the year to keep me focused on the direction I believe God wants me to take for the next twelve months. Leading up to one new year, a phrase kept coming to me. I started hearing it everywhere. In sermons. In books. Even in commercials. And it's not a typical goal-oriented phrase to motivate me to grow in Christ, like most years' were. My focus statement for the year became: *rest assured*.

There's a lot to be said for this phrase. The year prior, I found myself trying to fix too many dilemmas in attempting to provide for my own needs. I ended up "worrying my prayers" rather than walking in complete faith.* I wasn't stirred up in my worry, but it was a silent pressure always weighing on me.

Rest assured is a different kind of rest. It isn't a blind rest or a doubt-filled, tossing-and-turning type of rest. No, God wants me to *rest assured* that he's handling my life. *Rest assured* that he is in control. *Rest assured* that if he leads me to do something, he will equip me for the challenge. And *rest assured* that I don't have to be involved in every good opportunity that comes my way. I knew all those concepts already, but I'm not sure I was really living them. So, this was my challenge, and I chose to accept it. Would you like to join me?

> Less striving, struggling, achieving. More BE-ing. And when we add "B" to "less" we get *bless*!

Rest assured, Jesus has it covered.

How blessed the man you train, God, the woman you instruct in your Word, Providing a circle of quiet within the clamor of evil, while a jail is being built for the wicked. God will never walk away from his people, never desert his precious people. Rest assured that justice is on its way and every good heart put right.
(Psalm 94:12–15 MSG)

A World of Less

When I served for over thirty years as a pastor's wife, I often struggled with the gravity of not helping everyone needing help. I couldn't do it all. I prayed for more energy, more helpers, more techniques to reach those in need. Instead, I realized I needed to pray for *less*. What does *less* look like in a world of *more*? Less striving, struggling, achieving. More BE-ing. And when we add "B" to "less," we get *bless!*

---

* James 1:5–8 MSG

During the PAUSE

Pray

Oh Father, how often have you whispered in my ear to be still, and I buried your instructions with activity and noise? Change the go-to of my heart during stress from being busy to being still.

Adjust

I will modify my tendencies to make room for God's still small voice to be heard.

Undertake

I will start the process of learning to rest and experience the assurance that comes from waiting.

Seek

I will look for signs of overdoing it so I can stop before it overtakes my thoughts and time.

Evaluate

I will weigh out when it's time to do much versus the times I need to do nothing.

QUOTE: "But when you trust the Lord God to give you the next step, when you wait in humility upon Him, *He* will open the doors or close them, and you'll get to rest and relax until He says, 'Go.'" –Charles R. Swindoll[14]

ME in the RAW: I'm not looking to relax. I need to get on with my life already!

ME in the SPIRIT: Father, I love you enough to wait. Fill me with your faith. Help me to trust more than I worry and to wait more than I hurry.

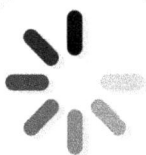

Chapter Eleven

FAITHFUL OR FAITH-FILLED?

F aithful is such a good word. Devoted, dedicated, loyal, consistent, true. But when we change the last part of that word to *filled,* "faith-filled," we see a whole new world open up and perhaps a way to endure our current situation. What changes in us when we're filled with faith? Our perspective. Our motives. Our actions. We see changes in others, too, because being faith-filled is contagious.

When our overflow of faith splashes onto them, maybe they are a little more inspired, motivated, mentored, and encouraged. It produces fruit such as peace, hope, and love. So, if I can only be one—faithful or faith-filled—I think I will take the second. And then, really, the first one will be a certain outcome anyway, won't it?

Filled Donuts

Anything that's filled sure sounds better than something that's full, doesn't it? Full can sometimes make me miserable (and long for my stretchy sweatpants). Then there's *filled.* Makes me think of decadence. Options. Jelly filled. Bavarian cream filled. I'm a happy gal!

When I was a little girl, the neighbor lady took me to a bakery. Once there, I beheld an entire donut counter with a variety of delicious doughy confections. I'm surprised my eyes didn't bug out of my head. The ones that caught my attention were the ones filled with yumminess. I came out of that shop with my very first cream horn. I'm sure there was powdered sugar everywhere!

Childlike Faith

Just as children love jelly-filled donuts, they love book-filled libraries. One time I came upon Mr. Book while checking out books. Mr. Book is not a human but rather a friendly robot. Two-year-old Wesley approached Mr. Book tentatively and was greeted with, "Hi, what's *your* name?"

With daddy's help, Wesley gave his name and said he was two years old. They had a sweet discussion, during which Wesley stared in utter amazement at the creature before him. Then he picked up some books to take home and "read." What Wesley didn't know was that there was a kind gentleman positioned in another part of the room with a headset. He spoke to each young child as they entered the library. He made their visit a personal, individual experience. Some walked away skeptical, others were afraid, but most were thrilled.

Being faith-filled is contagious.

The Bible says we are to have childlike faith.* We need to approach God and know that he *is* without having to know how he works or why he speaks to us so personally. Just as Mr. Book was not limited to the robotic, box-shaped book, our God cannot be placed in a box. We will never be able to figure him out because his ways are not our ways.

When we pray, who do we envision? Some think of a grand-fatherly Santa Claus figure in the clouds. Others think of a judge garbed in a black robe. Some think of Jesus with children on his lap or speaking to the multitudes from a boat. There are those who see Jesus still on the cross, although we realize he is no longer suffering. The great thing is we do not have to all share the same

---

*   Matthew 18:3

experience when we pray. But we all must come with the faith of a child. A faith that does not waver. Faith is believing in what we cannot see. Trust.

Just like the readers in the library, some will walk away skeptical, others will be afraid, but most will know a thrill that cannot be explained with mortal words.

Mr. Book wanted to inspire young readers to desire to be voracious readers. Our God desires us to be avid, insatiable readers of *the* Book.

Will you come to him today, in faith, believing that he is?

And it is impossible to please God without faith. Anyone who wants to come to him must believe that God exists and that he rewards those who sincerely seek him. (Hebrews 11:6)

The View from Others

I asked friends on Facebook:

> When you see the compound word *faith-filled*, what comes to mind? Does it differ from the word faithful? What does *filled* in general mean to you? I'm writing a chapter for my next book about this topic, and how it pertains to when our lives feel like they are on hold, and we are left waiting.[15]

Here are the responses:

Stephenie Hovland:

> I love that word. Different from faithful, which to me means being steadfast and devoted. Faith-filled means what I do comes from a life filled with faith. The natural outpouring and overflowing of God's grace for me flows through me.

Lee Walker Merrill:

> I think of faith-filled meaning full to overflowing with faith, even in hard times. Faithful, to me, is a synonym for trustworthy or dependable.

Denise Ackerman:

I have not heard the term faith-filled used before. My definition of faithful means to stay the course throughout life's ups and downs, twists and turns. Like a ship that has set its course. Faith-filled, is more a description of one's attitude and beliefs. A believer who does not doubt or become fearful when facing life's trials and tests.

Joanie Shawhan:

When I think of faithful, I think of honoring God no matter the circumstances. I think of God as honoring his Word and promises to us. When I think of faith-filled, I think of a person who trusts God in the face of adversity with joy.

Lisa-Anne Valentine Wooldridge:

In our lives, we often have empty places and lonely spaces, but if we are faith-filled, hope streams in and fills the gaps and leads us forward with purpose and courage.

Becki James:

To be faith-filled is to allow one's faith to direct all aspects of one's life—from thoughts to action.

TLC Nielsen:

Faithful feels like a longer-term word, while faith-filled feels more present tense to me. I am faithful to my Lord and Savior, Jesus Christ but have wonderful faith-filled moments along the way.

Jill Stanish:

Faithful, to me, is reliability, constancy, and trustworthiness that may or may not have anything to do with "faith." Faith-filled is when our habits, relationships, behaviors demonstrate a complete reliance upon and trust in God.

Gina Stinson:

> To me, the action of faithfulness is a result of being faith-filled. I can be faithful to God because within me, I have the record of a lifetime of his faithfulness to me. These seeds of his faithfulness strengthen my own desire to be faithful.

A New Perspective

How can we cope with this current wait? By increasing our faith. God isn't punishing us for not having enough faith. However, having more faith will certainly help us get our eyes off the problem and onto the Peace Speaker. Just as love is a choice instead of a feeling, faith is a choice instead of a feeling.

> *If we are faithless, He remains faithful [true to His word and His righteous character], for He cannot deny Himself.*
>
> (2 Timothy 2:13 AMP)

When we admit our faith is dim, we can access more by going to our faithful God.

During the PAUSE

Pray

Oh Papa God, in this current waiting time, please fill me to the brim with faith—enough to endure feeling on hold and forgotten. Help this faith produce fruit, even when I feel barren.

Adjust

I will swap out my defeatist view of my circumstances and instead operate in faith-filled hope.

Undertake

I will make my faith a present-tense practice rather than a waiting-for-a-better-time procrastination.

Seek

I will look for a verse in the Bible that will help me hold on to my shaking, uncertain faith.

Evaluate

I will examine my source of faith and determine on what I'm basing my current level of trust.

QUOTE: "Living a faith-filled life is always a work-in-progress, a life-long journey." –Kathryn Shirey[16]

ME in the RAW: I want the progress without the work, the long life without the journey!

ME in the SPIRIT: A faith-filled focus is the only work in progress that is worth perfecting over the course of my entire life.

Chapter Twelve

LIFE IN THE SLOW COOKER

Are you treading water in the deep end of the slow cooker—waiting on God to work out your mess to create a yummy outcome? Come up with your own *wait-and-see* recipe, and you'll learn how ingredients improve when cooked under low heat for a long time. They marinate and meld, yielding a better result due to the process. Tender and flavorful. When we see waiting as an ingredient to a better outcome, we feel more productive as we live life on hold.

Don't Slow Me Down

My Aunt Verna Jean is a fast walker. She has always been able to walk circles around most people, and she gets a lot done with her hurry-up-and-don't-wait pace. I think I've inherited that gene. A lot of good things happen when I'm at breakneck speeds. I brainstorm with clients while I'm fast-walking because it stimulates a part of my brain that works best when my feet are also at work. Despite my disabling health conditions, I get more to-do tasks done than average because I work faster, not harder. But there are some significant flaws to this way of life.

I've lost track of how many injuries I've sustained because I don't want to slow down. Multiple broken toes from stubbing them while going from here to there in a nanosecond. One time, the entire front end of my foot folded under on itself as I stepped, tearing an important tendon in my foot. That one ended up causing over a year in physical therapy, surgery, setbacks, and a wheelchair. Another time, I broke my heel (which I hear is hard to do—I have a gift!) from missing a stair step in my hurry to get to a restaurant. That meal didn't happen. Instead, I got an ambulance ride.

> When we see waiting as an ingredient to a better outcome, we feel more productive as we live life on hold.

There are other ways I go fast if I'm not careful. The first time I was pulled over by an officer was the first day of driving a brand-new Dodge Colt with the best standard transmission I ever had. I raced through those gears, unaware that with each shift, my car went faster. Not a wise move driving through town. Thankfully, I was let off with a warning when he saw my paperwork and sympathized that I was still getting used to the way the vehicle handled. Now I'm more cautious watching that speedometer because I really don't want to be pulled over again.

I come by the fast walking honestly—through Aunt Verna Jean's genes. The speeding? Not a clue.

I guess you can tell it's hard to slow me down—yet necessary. And waiting is one way I'm learning to slow down. I can't say I always love it, though—especially when those pauses aren't voluntary.

Waiting Makes Me Impatient

I'm an impatient person, so I don't like admitting that I know waiting makes things better. What happens when I don't wait for that hot pizza to cool down before I take the first bite? I burn the roof of my mouth. The wait is part of the process, even though it seems like a waste of time.

My mom chides me for walking too fast. She has a point—just look at my injury track record. But walking from point A to point B is a waste of time. I just want to get there already.

Back in my parsonage-dwelling days, speed created an accident. I had my arms full of shoes to return to the closet before the housecleaner arrived. She only came twice a month, so things piled up in between times. I was one of those who had to straighten up before she could clean up.

So, there I was rushing through the house on a deadline (before she gets here!), and my slipper socks made contact with the slick bathroom tile, and—you guessed it—I slipped and fell.

On the way down, I did a proper cheerleading split. One leg in the closet, the other in the commode area. My body, not liking the idea of doing the splits, rebelled, and I tumbled over into yet another ouchie position. *SIGH*. All because I didn't want to take the time to slow down.

My hurry-up moment led to a lot of slow-down moments until the injuries healed. So yes, I acknowledge

> **The wait is part of the process, even though it seems like a waste of time.**

that it is good to wait, to slow down, to let the delay happen so when the desired outcome gets here, we're ready for it.

Not Time Yet

My Boston terrier Hettie doesn't like to wait any more than I do. Every single day she has a routine that involves getting treats at certain times. She gives me the look when she thinks it's time for her jerky. She has learned to recognize it, but not like it, when I say the words: "Not time yet." When I say it, I sometimes think of the thing I'm waiting for, and tell myself, *Kathy, not time yet!*

The other phrase I tell Hettie (and myself) is, "You have to wait." If I gave Hettie her treat before it was time, soon she would start to beg for it more and more. And she wouldn't learn to wait. She would think she gets whatever she wants, whenever she wants it. To prevent that, I have a set time of day to give her what she wants. In between times, she has to wait.

A pregnant woman would hate for her child to arrive as soon as she found out she was pregnant. She wouldn't be ready yet. And a writer wouldn't benefit from sitting down to write a book and getting up five minutes later with a completed manuscript. There is growth in the process. Improvement. Waiting makes us impatient, but instead, we need to use the time to anticipate the outcome and to figure out if there are learning opportunities before it's time yet.

> We need to use the time to anticipate the outcome and to figure out if there are learning opportunities before it's time yet.

One way I like making myself slow down is by taking nature photography, especially macro shots of flowers. I love making myself stop, resisting my usual fast pace, in order to get the right angle, lighting, and frame for the perfect image.

This quote from Karen Wingate is the perfect prayer for while we wait. "Lord, help me work with you in the wait so I will be at my best when your answer comes. Prepare me so I can be ready to acknowledge you as the Giver of the gift."[17]

> *And so, dear friends, while you are waiting for these things to happen, make every effort to be found living peaceful lives that are pure and blameless in his sight.*
> (2 Peter 3:14)

While You Wait

Take some time to ponder these questions.

- What was the biggest "wait-and-see" life event for you? How did it turn out?

- Discuss a current "wait-and-see" moment you are going through. What are you learning?
- What encourages you to hold on when you feel you have more questions than answers?
- Why is *hope* so essential when you are in a holding pattern?
- Why do you think God delays in answering our prayers and fixing our messes?
- How has God surprised you when he responded in a different way than you prayed?
- What have you learned about yourself in this process?

> I will look for ways to add slow moments to my fast-paced life.

When I look at a Bible verse in several versions, it gives me different nuances of the message. Take a look at Habakkuk 2:3.

Habakkuk 2:3 (TLB)
But these things I plan won't happen right away. Slowly, steadily, surely, the time approaches when the vision will be fulfilled. If it seems slow, do not despair, for these things will surely come to pass. Just be patient! They will not be overdue a single day!

Habakkuk 2:3 (NLT)
This vision is for a future time. It describes the end, and it will be fulfilled. If it seems slow in coming, wait patiently, for it will surely take place. It will not be delayed.

Habakkuk 2:3 (MSG)
This vision-message is a witness pointing to what's coming. It aches for the coming—it can hardly wait! And it doesn't lie. If it seems slow in coming, wait. It's on its way. It will come right on time.

During the PAUSE

Pray

Oh, Master Chef of my life. Help me slow down so the ingredients have the opportunity to come together in flavors that are a sweet savor to your tastebuds.

Adjust

I will continue to modify my mindset so my tachometer isn't constantly redlining life.

Undertake

I will welcome the slow cooker life and focus on the scrumptious recipes it creates.

Seek

I will look for ways to add slow moments to my fast-paced life.

Evaluate

I will ask myself often why I'm in such a big hurry.

QUOTE: "I do not know why there is this difference, but I am sure that God keeps no one waiting unless He sees that it is good for him to wait. When you do enter your room, you will find that the long wait has done you some kind of good which you would not have had otherwise. But you must regard it as waiting, not as camping. You must keep on praying for light: and of course, even in the hall, you must begin trying to obey the rules which are common to the whole house. And above all you must be asking which door is the true one; not which pleases you best by its paint and paneling." –C.S. Lewis[18]

ME in the RAW: Beggars can't be choosers! Just give me any open door, and I'll rush through it so fast I won't have time to deliberate or doubt.

ME in the SPIRIT: If waiting helps to better me, or to grow someone else, or to improve the flavor of a future situation, then I'm willing to wait it out, knowing God has only the best intentions.

Chapter Thirteen

FIXATED DOESN'T FIX IT

W e all have this terrible tendency to "rubberneck." We drive toward a car accident and see something horrible. Yes, we should look away, but there's an unexplainable urge to keep staring. That same human propensity causes us to fixate so long on problems we can't focus on anything else. It takes an intentional re-focus to endure the wait.

Vision

I'll never forget how I discovered I needed glasses. My first clue was in junior high. The teacher sat me in the back of the class because I was one of the good girls. She kept the troublemakers closer to the front to keep her eyes on them. The problem with being in the back of the room was that I couldn't make out what the teacher wrote on the chalkboard. (Yes, that was back when we thought a green board rather than a blackboard was a modern invention for chalk. Dry-erase boards and SMART Boards were only concepts like the Jetson's futuristic food and transportation.) I couldn't read the teacher's notes, but I figured everyone else had the same problem.

Then the nurse called us one by one to her office for a mandatory eye exam. Do they even offer these anymore? That was the same year they checked us for scoliosis.

Next thing I knew, my parents received a note from the school. For a fleeting moment, we all wondered what I did to get in trouble. But I was a good girl, remember?

> We fixate so long on problems we can't focus on anything else. It takes an intentional refocus to endure the wait.

The note ended up being a notice from the nurse that I was nearsighted and needed to go to an eye doctor. This was a new thing for our family. None of the others wore glasses.

Mom got the name of an ophthalmologist in a town about forty-five minutes away because our small town didn't offer an eye doctor. Trips out of town were a big deal back then! Father, Brother, Mother, and I all loaded up into the car for the appointment. I'll never forget how out of focus everything was when the assistant dilated my eyes so the doctor could look at my retinas. I thought the world around me was blurry before, but now it was downright fuzzy! Not thinking, we went to the optical store right after the appointment, and I had to rely on Mom to help me pick out glasses—I could barely see straight. Fortunately, she has good taste and didn't lead me astray.

Before I knew it, I was sporting the latest aviator glasses with photochromic changing lenses. The doctor warned that I'd have a headache at first—once everything was back in focus—so I'd actually have to train my eyes to adjust to seeing correctly.

I first tried to focus on a tree in the distance. Without the glasses, I knew the tree was there, but that was about it. When I slipped on my aviators, I could see every branch, every leaf. *You mean this is what we were supposed to see?* The glasses brought everything in the distance into focus. Brighter. Crisper. In detail. Wow! The doctor was right—I did have a headache while my eyes adjusted to the new visual input. But it was so worth it to discover this whole new world.

Isn't that just like life? We have to work at seeing our circumstances and attitudes correctly. It might even hurt us at first while we adjust to a new perspective. But it's worth it to view our situations clearly. What might a little added clarity bring to your *pause*? When you alter your view of God, you'll alter your view of your circumstances.

Messed Up

My husband says I'm messed up. When we watch an action show on TV, I can take it when they show blood and guts. But only if it's *human* blood and guts. (Well . . . fake stage blood and guts.) But if there's even a hint that an animal might get hurt, I'm pleading with the television, "Don't hurt the puppy!" I just can't take it. And if I come to a commercial raising awareness and funds for neglected and abused animals, I have to click the remote to fast-forward or mute it. My heart can't handle those sad pictures paired with the Sarah McLachlan song "Angel." I have to look away.

In one of our early ministries, a church member had an odd sort of show-and-tell at his house instead of board games. He whipped out his black and white photo collection of terrible train and automobile wrecks. He worked as a first responder, and part of his job was to document the accident scene by taking pictures. The photos were graphic and horrible.

> What we focus on is what we feed, and what we ignore is what we starve. So, are we feeding our problems or starving them?

But for some reason, we found ourselves staring at the carnage rather than turning away. Sort of like those rubberneckers who slow down traffic to look at an accident on the side of the road as they drive by. That's how *additional* accidents happen. People should look away, but their eyes are glued to the bad news. And we do the same thing with life stuff—we focus on the bad when we'd be better off if we diverted our attention to something else.

What Are You Dwelling On?

Even though we feel we have no control over our thoughts, we really do. What we focus on is what we feed, and what we ignore is what we starve. So, are we feeding our problems or starving them? When we dwell on the problem (which is human nature), it grows. When we dwell on the solution, we might find our way out of the problem, but we might try to do it in our own strength. Then we mess things up, and we create more messes.

> What boulder could you plow through if you realized God could pulverize it instantly?

But when we dwell on Christ (and *in* Christ)—what a difference! Then the problems fade away. The solutions come to us like aha! moments. And the sting of the wait doesn't hurt nearly as much because we're with Jesus. Yes, dwelling on and in Christ is the answer. As we spend time with God in conversation, our minds are likely to wander. Don't beat yourself up when that happens. God understands how we're wired. But he loves it when we take those mind-wandering (and wondering) thoughts captive—lassoing them and reeling them back in, so we can resume our chat with him.

There are so many excellent Bible verses about this mental discipline that it's vital to camp out here for just a bit.

Top 7 Tips to Fix Your Focus

1. **Focus on Jesus instead of on your problem.** Who is Jesus? He is the pioneer and perfecter of my faith. How small is my trial compared to what Jesus faced? He endured the shame of the cross before sitting down next to God's throne.*

2. **Feel like praising again with a God-focus.** *Why are you down in the dumps, dear soul? Why are you crying the blues? Fix my eyes on God—soon I'll be praising again. He puts a smile on my face. He's my God* (Psalm 42:5, 11 MSG).

3. **Look straight ahead and focus on the future rather than the past.**† Don't allow something that hurt you in the past to continue to mess up your life. Instead, embrace what God has in store for you moving forward.

4. **Retreat to a state of being rather than doing.** *Here's what I want you to do: Find a quiet, secluded place so you won't be tempted to role-play before God. Just be there as simply and honestly as you can manage. The focus will shift from you to God, and you will begin to sense his grace.* Matthew 6:6 MSG).

5. **Confess self-focused obsessions.** Being aware of any self-absorbed tendencies and being heartbroken about them leads to turning away from them. *Those who think they can do it on their own end up obsessed with measuring their own moral muscle but never get around to exercising it in real life. Those who trust God's action in them find that God's Spirit is in them—living and breathing God! Obsession with self in these matters is a dead end; attention to God leads us out into the open, into a spacious, free life. Focusing on the self is the opposite of focusing on God. Anyone completely absorbed in self ignores God, ends up thinking more about self than God. That person ignores who God is and what he is doing. And God isn't pleased at being ignored* (Romans 8:5–8 MSG).

---

*   Hebrews 12:2
†   Proverbs 4:25

6. **Switch from a focus on the temporary to a focus on the eternal.** It's tempting to fixate on what we don't like about *now* rather than investing our energy in a faith that hopes in a *future* with God's fingerprints all over it.*

7. **Press on despite the pit stops.** Life might be the pits, but it doesn't have to stop us.†

Powdered Rocks and Dirt Clods

They say in life we have to carry on, but there are times when the good and the bad all get jumbled up, and it's hard to keep plowing forward. We push the plow, we point it in the right direction, but we get stuck in the rut, or we want to back up and do it again to get a straighter line. Another challenge with these life-plow moments is when the blade strikes a rock. I have to remind myself to ignore these obstructions and plow through.

> I will get my spiritual eyes checked and change my lenses to ensure my vision is optimal.

They aren't the solid stones I think they are—they're just dirt clods—mere *powder* in God's hands.

What boulder could you plow through if you realized God could pulverize it instantly? Powdered rocks—not much to fear, is there? Maybe we wouldn't be stuck in those field ruts if we acted in faith and fixed our eyes on the end of the row ahead rather than the problems beneath the surface.

It's all about fixing our eyes on the right target. Not rubber-necking to focus on the problem as long as possible, but dogged determination to keep our focus, and our faith, on the one who can take care of it all in a way that draws us closer to him and helps us continue to fulfill his purpose in our lives—to his glory.

---

* 2 Corinthians 4:18
† Philippians 3:12–14

During the PAUSE

Pray

Father, you deserve all my focus. I confess I struggle with the temptation to fixate on the problems rather than to fix my eyes on you. Help me not miss out on a God-moment because I've gotten bogged down with something that won't even matter for eternity.

Adjust

I will get my spiritual eyes checked and change my lenses to ensure my vision is optimal. I'll ask, "Is this better or worse?" about each issue until I come up with a biblical prescription that accomplishes the best results.

Undertake

I will invest in someone else the next time I feel a self-focus infection coming on. I'll figure out a way to be a blessing to them, and in doing so, it will also help the issues in my own life fade a bit.

Seek

I will consider how God sees this situation and endeavor to adopt that same perspective.

Evaluate

I will make a list of times in the past week I've had my focus on something that would defeat me rather than propel me toward a better outcome. I'll evaluate a better way to deal with those same issues in the future.

QUOTE: "When one door closes another always opens, but we usually look so long, so intently and so sorrowfully upon the closed door that we do not see the one that has opened." –Author unknown[19]

ME in the RAW: In my life, not only does the door slam shut, but the windows are barricaded with storm shutters, and someone turns out the lights. The power goes out, and I hunker down for a storm.

ME in the SPIRIT: The Heavenly Architect designed multiple doors and windows, styled to open and close at his command, and all I have to do is focus on him to have a joy that surpasses temporary happiness.

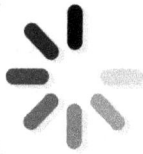

Chapter Fourteen

THE CHANGING ROOM

Have you ever selected several articles of clothing to try on in the changing room, only to walk away without a single option going home with you? It can seem like a lot of work with not a lot of results. But when you take in the right choices to begin with, you can come out of the changing room transformed, ready to embrace a new life. Don't dread the changing room—it's there to help you find the perfect fit.

New Attitude

Once upon a time, my dream job offered me a position, and it changed my life. I toted my writing portfolio to an area weekly newspaper and boldly asked for a job. (I don't know what got into me!) I found out they needed a copyeditor for the entire newspaper, plus a *faith and values* editor/writer. They could combine the two into one position if I proved I had what it took to do the job. They liked what I wrote, but was I editor material?

I didn't have a journalism degree or paid experience working for a newspaper. But I'd written for several newspapers and took journalism in high school. (Reading that now, I see how lame my claim to have experience must have sounded to them.) I had edited books for authors, which is different than newspaper editing. I told them I knew the distinctions between the AP Style Guide and Chicago Manual of Style, and if they tested me on editing, I'd show them I could do the job. So, they sent a very long editing exam and gave several hours to complete it. The next day, I got the job!

> Don't dread the changing room—it's there to help you find the perfect fit.

Their confidence in me caused *me* to have confidence in myself. I purchased a professional wardrobe, and my stylist gave me a new hairdo. Each time I made a change, I had extra spring in my step. A new attitude! This changing room experience was more than merely finding clothing fit for the job. It was about finding *myself* fit for the job.

Even though I hate going into the changing room (I'd rather simply buy clothing and know it fits), I realize there's value in taking the time to do it right. And I just might walk out of that changing room a new person—transformed!

The changing-room experiences in our lives do the same thing. We might not like how the changing room slows down our desired outcome, but we sure do like it when we finally get to leave, stepping into the next season of our lives.

One of life's changing rooms is when we need to transform a mess we've made of our lives (or someone else created for us) into something worthwhile.

Transforming a Crumbled Mess

What do you do with mistakes and leftovers? Why, you make a trifle, of course. I first made a sugar-free coffee cake into little mini-Bundts. But even with my best attempt to coat the pans, the cakes stuck. I was left with a crumbled mess. Crumbled mess accidents can turn into a yummy "on purpose" dessert. I surveyed my supplies.

I found two individual pudding cups of sugar-free dulce de leche (sort of like a caramel-flavored pudding with caramel on

114

top). I also found Cool
Whip Lite. So, I mixed
the pudding into the
whipped topping.

Next, I looked for
a pie filling or canned
fruit. I found crushed

> **The delays we experience aren't added to our lives to destroy us but to transform us.**

pineapple in juice. So, then I started the layering process. Half of
the crumbled cake mess went first. Then pineapple plus juice to
moisten the dry cake. Next, the pudding whip. Then the rest of
the mess-take (I mean cake) and then the rest of the whipped con-
coction. Then some changing room incubation time in the fridge.

Not only was it a delicious way to turn crumbs into a treat, but
it also reminded me to do the same with my life messes. I wonder
how it will turn out. The trifle turned out great—and I think the
life will too!

The delays we experience aren't added to our lives to destroy us
but to transform us. And the wait doesn't delay God's purpose—it
fulfills it.

Put On

Just like we put on clothing in the changing room to see if it transforms us, the Bible gives us spiritual clothing to put on.

> *Throw off your old sinful nature and your former
> way of life, which is corrupted by lust and deception.
> Instead, let the Spirit renew your thoughts and
> attitudes. Put on your new nature, created to be like
> God—truly righteous and holy.*
> (Ephesians 4:22–24)

> *Put on all of God's armor so that you will be able to
> stand firm against all strategies of the devil.*
> (Ephesians 6:11)

> *Therefore, put on every piece of God's armor so you will
> be able to resist the enemy in the time of evil. Then*

*after the battle you will still be standing firm. Stand
your ground, putting on the belt of truth and the body
armor of God's righteousness. For shoes, put on the
peace that comes from the Good News so that you will
be fully prepared. In addition to all of these, hold up
the shield of faith to stop the fiery arrows of the devil.*

(Ephesians 6:13–16)

It looks to me as if Paul wanted the Ephesian faith family to
go into the changing room and come out changed. What did they
need to do to be truly righteous and holy? They simply had to put
on their new nature. The one created to be like God in his holiness.
We aren't God, but he wants us to put on godly traits. Thankfully,
we aren't expected to do that in our own strength. If we did, it would
be in the flesh, and we know what a mess that makes. Instead, when
we are filled with the Spirit and allow his fruit to mature, getting
dressed in godliness is an inside job. How do we get filled with
the Spirit? By yielding our will to God's will and being connected to the vine (abiding in God).* Basically, it's when we quit having to go our own way.

> The wait doesn't delay God's purpose—it fulfills it.

God knows that those of us in a "pause" will face spiritual battle.
So, he provides clothing we can put on to fight the devil and endure the test. God's armor and his instruction to stand our ground
are just what we need to come out of the changing room truly
changed.

Paul also talks to the Colossians about putting on something
in order to change.

*Put on your new nature, and be renewed as you learn
to know your Creator and become like him.*

(Colossians 3:10)

---

* John 15:4–5

Becoming

We are carefully joined together in him, becoming a holy temple for the Lord.

(Ephesians 2:21)

And so we are transfigured much like the Messiah, our lives gradually becoming brighter and more beautiful as God enters our lives and we become like him.

(2 Corinthians 3:18 MSG)

I like the sound of the word *becoming*. It reminds me of a glamorous gal from the 1950s. Someone would say of them, "Aren't they becoming?" Another, "They are so becoming!" Or "That outfit is so becoming on them." Yes, they are stunning. Beautiful. But what are they becoming?

The truth is, the time we will be most becoming is when we have allowed God to be at work in us to become what he wants us to become. Transformation. And if we've learned anything during this waiting journey, it is the fact that God wants to use the pause as much as he wants to use the go. So, what will I put on to transform into the becoming person he wants me to be? How will I use this changing room experience to change *me*?

During the PAUSE

Pray

Help me select the right choices so this changing room experience transforms me, equipping me for what is up ahead. I lay aside my dread for this delay and praise you for dressing me in grace.

Adjust

I will adjust my attitude about my time in the changing room to anticipate the transformation that awaits rather than growing impatient with the time it takes to change.

Undertake

I will remove the soul clothes that don't become me—that don't help me become Christlike.

Seek

I will seek out the best "clothing" to take to the changing room with me so I'm spiritually clothed in the godly virtues needed as I wait.

Evaluate

I will think through how God wants to transform me as I wait. I will put on the mind of Christ so I can become more like him.

QUOTE: "I want to change my circumstances. God wants to change me." –Rick Warren[20]

ME in the RAW: If I promise to change, *then* can I get what I want?

ME in the SPIRIT: Knowing God has designed me for something more, something better, something that takes time while I transform—I will wait for the change before I rush to where I want to be.

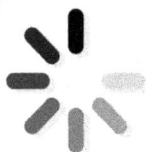

Chapter Fifteen

SOMETHING BETTER THAN THIS

Often, it's hard to know what to pray when you're in a holding pattern. Waiting can lead to either the worst environment for prayer or the best environment. One way to revolutionize your prayers is not only to be transparent with God but then to add a new request for something *better* at the end of your prayers. You will begin to be alert to God's blessings in your life when you ask God to bring about something better than *this*.

April Showers Bring May Flowers

I love May flowers, but April showers can get old. Rainy days are great when curled up with a good book but not so much fun when I need to get out. And I cringe to admit this sign of getting older: I ache more when it rains. But I can endure the storms because I know what's coming next. May flowers! What we're going through today is merely progress steps toward the beauty of tomorrow's blossoms.

In the middle of Russ's eight-month unemployment, I had to remind myself that the waiting days weren't wasting days unless I wasted them. Are you waiting on something today? Maybe you're not seeing much progress. The concern or desire of your heart isn't experiencing relief yet. Today isn't wasted unless *we* waste it. Each day always has an opportunity for growth. God has a plan for the quiet place as much as he has a plan for active progress.

> You will be alert to God's blessings in your life when you ask God to bring about something better than *this*.

When we wait for a circumstance to change so life can happen, we waste our days—our very breath. Start living today. Tell yourself, "Life starts NOW!" At whatever age, whatever weight, whatever financial situation, whatever relationship status, whatever health ordeal. Life starts now! The day we stop truly living is the day we begin to die.

Good, Better, Best

God is at work to do something special both *during* and at the end of our wait. It's sort of like waiting for Christ to return or heaven to come—we know the end of our wait is going to be special. But God wants the time while we're waiting to be significant too.

Or, to use another analogy, when you're feeling on hold, remind yourself that you're just at the starting line of a race. It looks like it could be a marathon, but maybe God will allow it to be a sprint. And he wants you to enjoy the journey as much as the destination. But oh—the destination! It will eventually be an amazing celebration. That's why we can pray for something better than *this* (whatever *this* is in your world). *The Message* paraphrases the words of Jesus in John 10:10 this way: *I came so they can have real and eternal life, more and better life than they ever dreamed of.*

Hope Is a Surprise Party

Have you ever been stuck in a spot between stop and go and wondered why God wasn't giving you a green light? It's tempting to lose hope, abandon faith, and drop your trust in him when he doesn't act on your prayers in a timely fashion. (His timetable is different than ours.)

I found myself in that situation. We had moved to a temporary dwelling, in a temporary town, in a temporary state, until we knew where God was moving us for my husband's next calling. I called it "just passing through." Another pastor's wife told me she calls it "the meantime of in-between time." When I heard that, I realized that God isn't mean. Like I've mentioned before, I'm encouraged to know that God somehow removes the "mean" from *meantime*. We might feel as if it's mean time, like bully time. But if I divide the letters in the word *meantime*, it becomes *meant* (for) *I* (and) *me*. So, these meantime moments can seem very mean to us, but maybe they are meant for us. I know the pause won't last forever, but it already feels like it's been an eternity.

> May God give you something to hang your hope on.

Here's what I wrap my mind around that gives me peace. It's as if God is planning a surprise party for us, and we don't know the *when* or the *where*. It wouldn't be much of a surprise party if we did, now, would it? So, as awful as this feels, we know it does get better than this!

Something Better than This

When you don't know what to pray during your wait, consider asking God for something else:

- Relief
- Release
- Restructuring
- Reassurance
- Rest

Try this prayer formula on for size: "God, please _____ [help me find a doctor, help me find a job, etc.] or something better."

121

And while you wait for your something better to appear, be on the lookout for an everyday surprise right now. God drops those into our lives to give us assurance as we wait. May God give you something to hang your hope on.

If you are going through a rough patch or are feeling overwhelmed, here's something you might find helpful. I like to remind myself: I'm glad God isn't confined to the box of my imagination. He's bigger than even that. Which means he can take care of even this. If Jesus is powerful enough to come back to life after being crucified, he is powerful enough to take care of any of my concerns, including this one.

Car Prayers

Today as I drove to my destination, I dragged myself to God's presence in prayer. I say *dragged* because I was a bit ashamed. I didn't like how I was feeling. My attitudes and emotions were embarrassing and even shameful, considering the depth of faith I think I have.

God didn't let me berate myself for long, though. He gave me peaceful assurance that he loved me regardless. A reminder that he has seen it all and heard it all, and his love for me isn't based on how I'm dealing with my current trial. He just wanted to spend time with me. I know we hear that a lot, but it doesn't mean we put it into practice. God helped me see what was at the root of my feelings and how those resolve when I spend time with him. The problem didn't resolve, but my perspective changed. God gave me that something better—it was simply spending time with him in a way that made me feel loved and cared for rather than judged and scolded.

So maybe your something better is God-and-me time. I returned home to the same problems but without the weight of them pressing on me. Instead, God did an inside job aimed right at my heart, and my mind discovered new thoughts in the process.

It Gets Better than This

I've gone through some yucky health issues. It seems like I collect them instead of fine jewelry! One of the times when I had to be on steroids for a year the doctors wanted to wean me off. Let's just say it wasn't a very fun process. Who knew the body quits making its own cortisone when given extra and has to learn to produce it all over again? During that "weaning" process, I had to rely on God even more than my everyday trust. There was extra pain. Withdrawal symptoms. You name it. But since I had gone through the weaning process a previous time, at least I could tell myself, "It does get better than this." I knew I just had to wait it out. Sounds like the theme of this book, doesn't it?

While I praise— the Spirit prays!

I found this in my journal, written during that weaning and waiting period:

> This week when I struggle to pray, I think of the Bible verse that says the Holy Spirit prays for us when we don't know how. That made me determine to praise God despite the sense of lack. Not to worry so much about asking for the daily bread of what I need next. To remind myself that the Spirit asks God for what I need when I'm at a loss for words. I came up with, "While I praise—he prays!" I can't remain speechless for long when I begin to praise God for all his wonderful attributes and character traits.

What would happen if you changed your prayers for praises? I'm not saying we should do that all the time because God does want to hear our requests, and he says we have not because we ask not. But when we don't know what to pray, let's determine to praise and let the Spirit be our prayer partner.

I found this paraphrase of Romans 8:22–28 from *The Message* that helped me as I waited out that awful steroid reduction plan. It says:

All around us we observe a pregnant creation. The difficult times of pain throughout the world are simply birth pangs. But it's not only around us; it's within us. The Spirit of God is arousing us within. We're also feeling the birth pangs. These sterile and barren bodies of ours are yearning for full deliverance. That is why waiting does not diminish us, any more than waiting diminishes a pregnant mother. We are enlarged in the waiting. We, of course, don't see what is enlarging us. But the longer we wait, the larger we become, and the more joyful our expectancy.

Meanwhile, the moment we get tired in the waiting, God's Spirit is right alongside helping us along. If we don't know how or what to pray, it doesn't matter. He does our praying in and for us, making prayer out of our wordless sighs, our aching groans. He knows us far better than we know ourselves, knows our pregnant condition, and keeps us present before God. That's why we can be so sure that every detail in our lives of love for God is worked into something good.

> My situation is ripe for God to create a wonder-working answer to prayer.

My wacky sense of humor had a heyday with that passage. I laughed within my soul and decided I was going to allow myself to get large. That's not something a woman says to herself every day! But it wasn't going to be the largeness of expansive thighs and breaking moans. It would be wordless sighs and aching groans, suitable for the Spirit to enter into the prayer conversation as our liaison and represent us to the One who can bring about something better. If not in this life, in the next.

During the PAUSE

Pray

May I use this waiting time to be real with you and see you at work in my life. Release me from this situation, or if not, deliver something even better, bringing glory to your name.

Adjust

Instead of feeling like I have a target on my back, I will change my perception to realize my situation is ripe for God to create a wonder-working answer to prayer.

Undertake

I will remind myself that God isn't mean in this meantime situation. It is in-between time.

Seek

I will seek what is good about my current situation while also learning to look for the "something better" that will happen in this life or the next.

Evaluate

I will consider what I've been holding back in my prayers and replace my whiny, wimpy prayers with bold prayers that live up to God's ability to deliver something better than this.

QUOTE: "Christ followers know that this—and the forthcoming troubles—are not the end of the story. Even though things are going to get far worse on the earth and trials will increase, what is happening now is just the beginning of getting to the good stuff. Ultimately, it's only going to get better. It's going to be sooo good." –Shana Schutte[21]

ME in the RAW: I'm tired of waiting for things to get better. How do we even know that good things come to those who wait? I want the good stuff now! I know there will be a good ending, but what about a good "middle"?

ME in the SPIRIT: May God help me pray in such a way that I sense he is at work in me and through me and will deliver an outcome that benefits his kingdom, in his time.

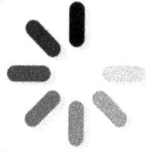

Chapter Sixteen

STOP WORRYING TO WORSHIP

When we wear blinders to block out distractions and focus on God with all his attributes, we can't help but worship. And when we worship, all else fades away. We must tune out even trials to truly worship. When we do that and revisit our challenges after worship, they never seem as big. Individual or corporate worship is a great default for worrying. It's like rebooting the heart and mind. You'll exit your time of worship with a fresh perspective.

Worship is Liberating

Worshiping the Lord is a favorite heart song of mine—even though I know it seems my health, work, family, and ministry take up the lion's share of my thoughts. Worship is so freeing, leaving behind pain, shackles, legalism, and expectations. And worship makes sure I let go of any *me* thoughts. Absence of self.

When we endure the wait of delay, we tend to fret. Fretting is uptight worrying. Stressing about something has never proven to accomplish a positive outcome. But often, it delays the end of waiting. We create more problems. We dig a deeper hole, and it takes longer to pull ourselves up out of the pit. Fretting only exhausts us as we fight against the wait—strength is depleted, and joy evaporates.

Worry is the opposite of faith. If faith opens the door for us to see God at work, worry closes that door. It causes us to lean on our own understanding rather than lean on God. Worry is the way our mind tries to solve the problem and unravel the solution at the same time due to all the what-ifs. It prepares for regret and doubt ahead of time. Worry is like trying to get to our destination on a treadmill. Worship is like running to our destination with Daddy at the finish line—so carefree, we can't even feel our feet on the track.

> **Worry is like trying to get to our destination on a treadmill.**

When we get in a hurry, we not only worry, we whine. There's a sense of impatient urgency. *Just do something already!* Even today, I've been whiny. I don't like the sound I make when I vocalize my frustrations. They are sort of like nasally complaints. I wonder if I crowd out the sense of God's presence in my life when I vent about unfulfilled wishes? I'm sure I do because my eyes aren't on him.

> *If you don't know what you're doing, pray to the Father. He loves to help. You'll get his help, and won't be condescended to when you ask for it. Ask boldly, believingly, without a second thought. People who "worry their prayers" are like wind-whipped waves. Don't think you're going to get anything from the Master that way, adrift at sea, keeping all your options open.*
>
> (James 1:5–8 MSG)

> *Even if you suffer for doing what is right, God will reward you for it. So don't worry or be afraid of their threats. Instead, you must worship Christ as Lord of your life. And if someone asks about your hope as a believer, always be ready to explain it.*
>
> (1 Peter 3:14–15)

Rick Warren says this about worry and worship:

> There are two alternatives when you feel pressured to be quiet about your faith in Christ: You can worry, or you can worship. That means you either panic or you pray. You either focus on the problem and the pressure and the persecution, or you can focus on God.
>
> You have to turn your attention away from the pressure you feel and turn it toward God. That's what worship is — focusing on God. When you face opposition, worship instead of worry.[22]

When we worship instead of worry, we express our trust in God to be so powerful that nothing, not even that thing we are tempted to worry about, can keep us from living the life

> **Worship displaces worry.**

God wants us to live. Worship reminds us of who God is. His bigness is in focus, and our problems look small in comparison.

> *For God is greater than our worried hearts and knows more about us than we do ourselves.*
>
> (1 John 3:20 MSG)

I wrote this in *The Grin Gal's Guide to Wellbeing*:

Steps to heart-and-soul peace

Live life in Christ Jesus and let go of what holds you back. God will grant peace, and that peace is what is available to guard your heart and mind. *Don't worry about anything; instead, pray about everything. Tell God what you need and thank him for all he has done. Then you will experience God's peace, which exceeds anything we can understand. His peace will guard your hearts and minds as you live in Christ Jesus* (Philippians 4:6–7).

1. **Go on a worry fast.** Each time a worry surfaces

129

in your mind, learn how to replace it with prayer and biblical self-talk.

2. **Pray with petitions and praises.** Petitions are those specific requests we confide to God. (I tell my friends I pray with TMI, but God doesn't see it that way. He loves to hear from me—too much information and all.) Let God know your concerns but also focus on praising him. Worship displaces worry.

3. **Focus on God's attributes.** When you read Scripture, search for a virtue or role of God—a characteristic trait. Hint: usually, this is something I value about God that I can't attain 100 percent in my humanness. Choose one attribute to focus on as you praise him during your personal worship time.

4. **Sense God's wholeness as you absorb his peace.** This peace is different than manmade peace. It contributes to heart-and-soul wellbeing. It quiets the upset and delivers rest, sort of like an antacid calms heartburn.[23]

Letting Go of Worry

We all know worry is self-destructive, but it's much easier to acknowledge it than to stop it. So, what steps can we take to get rid of the fret? *Be still in the presence of the Lord, and wait patiently for him to act. Don't worry about evil people who prosper or fret about their wicked schemes* (Psalm 37:7).

1. **Be still.** To be still means to truly rest in God, believing in faith that God's timing is worth the wait. When I need an example of this, I think about how Jesus slept during the storm on that boat while the others felt every toss and turn of the crashing waves. His ability to rest showed he trusted his Father even when the storms raged. If it's hard for me to

be still, and I'm fighting against it, I have to remind myself that nothing is too hard for God. When I replace "I've got this" with "God's got this!" then I can sense my heartbeat slowing down and my resistance easing off. I know that waking up during the night and catching myself fretting is the opposite of resting in God.

2. **Wait patiently for God to act.** You will know when the holding pattern has ended, and God's about to land the plane. And you'll know when it's premature to try to get on the ground—all that amounts to is a crash-landing without the running gear down. Patience is only developed during the wait, never in the rush. What happens when we wait impatiently? Whether we wait with patience or impatience, it takes just as long, but when we're impatient, we're miserable.

> God's timing is worth the wait.

3. **Don't keep track of others.** It's easy to get into the comparison game and wonder why other people aren't suffering. During the wait, it's easy to get worked up about life not being fair. We have no idea what is going on in their lives. If we find ourselves longing for what someone else seems to have, we are a long way off from being in a mindset to worship and wait.

> *Yet God has made everything beautiful for its own time. He has planted eternity in the human heart, but even so, people cannot see the whole scope of God's work from beginning to end.*
>
> (Ecclesiastes 3:11)

Reading "its own time" in that passage makes me realize that my desire to hurry something to get to what I want risks it being something less than the beautiful outcome God is creating in me.

When we can get to the place of choosing to trust instead of worry—trusting God's timing is perfect—we'll be able to see that his timing is beautiful, even. And that is the beginning of worship, isn't it?

During the PAUSE

Pray

Oh Father, how I want to hand over my worry and replace it with a heart and mind full of worship. You deserve my complete focus, not my fixated fears. I am astounded by your grace.

Adjust

I will substitute worship for worry, delights for doubts, and shining for whining.

Undertake

I will overhaul my thought-life by calling out each worry for what it is. It destroys worship.

Seek

I will seek God's face even when I'm ashamed to look at him.

Evaluate

I will evaluate why I think this worry is more rational than the opportunity to worship.

QUOTE: "The more you pray, the less you'll panic. The more you worship, the less you worry. You'll feel more patient and less pressured." –Rick Warren[24]

ME in the RAW: I'm not worried; I'm frustrated! I'm not panicked; I'm impatient!

ME in the SPIRIT: As I focus on the attributes of God in worship, the details of all else fades away. When I forget to fix my gaze on the Father, may my attitude of worship refocus me.

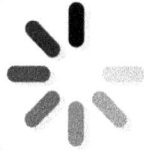

Chapter Seventeen

IS GOD ENOUGH?

Often the purpose of being put on hold is to learn a life lesson. After coming out of a waiting period, most will say that they learned the sufficiency of God—that he is enough. It may sound trite, but it's true, When God is all we have, God is all we need. It sometimes takes what seems like a delay to get our attention—to put us in a position where this truth of *enoughness* sinks in.

The Worry of Enough

If your husband has ever invited company over for dinner on a day when you planned to warm up leftovers, then you know the prayer of enough. Or if you're on vacation and catch yourself saying, "There's just never enough time to do everything I want to do." And if you've ever wanted to buy an ice cream cone from the change in your couch and car, you know the pressing desire of *enough*.

One falsehood we desperately believe is that once we learn the life lesson God wants us to understand through a situation, we will graduate from that lesson and won't have to deal with it again. We endure the wait, thinking it will be worth it all to not have to repeat that lesson. We don't want to leave the waiting room prematurely because that might mean we have to go through it all over again.

This principle isn't found in Scripture, and it doesn't play out in life. Life just happens. Every now and then, we have to revisit certain lessons. Maybe they are refresher courses. Maybe God wants to use us in the wait for someone else to learn a life lesson they'll need to equip them for a future circumstance. We can't possibly know the intricate tapestry of God's logic and logistics. All we can do is seek him during the wait and realize that he is enough, regardless if it's the first or the fifty-first time we've gone through it.

> We can't possibly know the intricate tapestry of God's logic and logistics.

During one of my waiting periods, my friend Peggy Still reminded me that God is my Protector, my Source, and my Security. She also suggested I read Proverbs 4:20–23, with the principle that his words are the key to life and bring health to the whole body. She said, "These truths that we hold on to carry us through the storm. Our goal is to be undaunted by anything that can pull us under."

> *My child, pay attention to what I say. Listen carefully to my words. Don't lose sight of them. Let them penetrate deep into your heart, for they bring life to those who find them, and healing to their whole body. Guard your heart above all else, for it determines the course of your life.*
>
> (Proverbs 4:20–23)

Enough Already

Each time another hit attempts to knock you off your feet, you probably feel like throwing your hands up in disgust and despair, exclaiming, "Enough already!" Enough pain. Enough delays. Enough worry. Enough rejection. Enough bad stuff to last a lifetime. One good thing to come from that futility is the act of surrender. Just like when a criminal lifts his hands in the air and says, "I give up—take me," we yield to our God to make all the difference when there's nothing within our power to make things better.

It's time to change the enough-already mindset to a different kind of enough. Instead of giving up—giving in. God is sufficient for this "Enough already!" moment. Even this one right now.

The Place of Enough

In this age of self-reliance, it's easy to forget how to rely on God for our needs. We want to be like the two-year-old who said, "I do it myself!" Often, we are brought to a place of waiting by having everything else stripped away until it feels like we have nothing left. But of course, we know that's not

> In this age of self-reliance, it's easy to forget how to rely on God for our needs.

true. Because we have God. He will never leave us or forsake us. Losing it all reminds us that our true resource is in God alone. He is our Provider. Our Comforter. Our *Enoughness* when all else is gone.

Always Enough

I looked for *enough* in the Bible and found more than enough. My first thought was how God gave the children of Israel enough manna for the day. Just the day. If they hoarded more, it would go bad. And to prepare for the Sabbath day, so they would rest, he gave them double, and it wouldn't spoil. That shows me God knows what I need, when I need it, and will supply it exactly on time so I can obey him in the act of gathering or in the act of resting. His resources are enough.

Not that we are sufficient of ourselves to think of anything as being from ourselves, but our sufficiency is from God.

(2 Corinthians 3:5 NKJV)

We like to think we're all that and a box of gluten-free crackers, but the truth is, we're nothing without God. So anytime we think we can take back control of our situation and fix it on our own, we fool ourselves. (And if we're honest, we're not even doing a good job of that.) That may sound like bad news, but it's really good news because it comes with the fact that God, in all his God-dom, *is* enough—*more* than enough for whatever we need.

> God is already at work on your behalf to create a future that will amaze you. A future filled with him.

But He has said to me, "My grace is sufficient for you [My lovingkindness and My mercy are more than enough—always available—regardless of the situation]; for [My] power is being perfected [and is completed and shows itself most effectively] in [your] weakness." Therefore, I will all the more gladly boast in my weaknesses, so that the power of Christ [may completely enfold me and] may dwell in me.

(2 Corinthians 12:9 AMP)

Focus on God's Sufficiency

We tend to fixate on what we're lacking in life—that thing we're waiting for to materialize. We pray. We wait. It's time to swap out our fixation. Instead, let's fix our eyes on Jesus, the author and finisher of our faith. We've discussed the concept of switching our focus before, but this time, we're going to adjust the focus lens to see a specific aspect of God. The object of our focus is that God is enough, and his provision is sufficient.

So we don't look at the troubles we can see now; rather, we fix our gaze on things that cannot be seen. For the things we see now will soon be gone, but the things we cannot see will last forever.

(2 Corinthians 4:18)

Fixing our eyes on Jesus, the pioneer and perfecter of faith.

(Hebrews 12:2 NIV)

We don't have to worry about whether we feel strong enough to face the day. In our weakness, there is a great gift. Grace. Enough of it to meet our needs. So, if you're having a crummy day and you just want to bury your head under the covers and wish it away, know that God's right there with you, and he's enough to help you make it through the day. He's already at work on your behalf to create a future that will amaze you. A future filled with him. And isn't that enough?

During the PAUSE

Pray

Oh Father, you are sufficient for all I need. You already know that, but I need to say it so that I go from knowing it to believing it. Thank you for providing for my need right on time.

Adjust

I will rely on you rather than on self or others to fulfill my life and fix my problems.

Undertake

I will remind myself that you never run out of the resources I need to live out my purpose.

Seek

I will be on the lookout for your *enoughness* whenever I am fixated on my lack.

Evaluate

I will examine my attitude and make sure I'm not allowing discontentment to sour my joy.

QUOTE: "Radical obedience to Christ is not easy . . . It's not comfort, not health, not wealth, and not prosperity in this world. Radical obedience to Christ risks losing all these things. But in the end, such risk finds its reward in Christ. And he is more than enough for us." –David Platt[25]

ME in the RAW: I've lost it all—where is God's provision for my current mess?

ME in the SPIRIT: I will embrace radical obedience to Christ, knowing the embrace he returns is enough.

Chapter Eighteen

PENSIVE PEACE

Others burn us or let us down when they disregard doing the right thing. Our expectations are dashed. After being hurt too many times, we begin to grow weary, to be leery, and to be teary. As we hold on to God, we gain his peace, but it's a pensive peace. We trust God, but we can't quite trust others anymore. How is your peace wilted when others disappoint you? How can you bolster that peace with a booster of God's assurance?

Bolstered Peace

When I was a young child, I feared fires, monsters, and the boogey-man. It always hit at night when I was supposed to be falling asleep. For example, I was convinced there was a monster under my bed. I imagined him piercing me with an arsenal of knives (or knife-like teeth!). I'm not sure how many times my mom reassured me that there was nothing under my bed but a little dust!

One way I overcame my fears during that period was to curl one arm above my head on the pillow for a regular night of dread. It was an imaginary security device. But on tormented nights, I arched both arms above my head, forming a virtual shield or halo of protection against whatever was threatening to harm me. In my childish thought process, I believed this was the way to signal to God that I needed his protection. And then I could fall asleep.

In my teen years, I replaced that pillow-halo ritual with prayer. A buttercream-colored bolster became my prayer altar.[26] Sometimes, I removed this large backrest pillow with arms from my bed, put it on the floor, and kneeled in front of it. There was something symbolic in doing this to let God know that I reverenced him, and I yielded to the control of his lordship.[27] When I unplugged from my life and focused on God alone during this prayer ritual, I regained the peace I needed to wait for my situation to improve. You could say he gave me *bolstered peace.*

> **God gives us *bolstered peace.***

The verb form of bolster means: boost, strengthen, reinforce, encourage, shore up, support, sustain.[28] When our lives are on hold, don't we need every single one of those benefits from the Lord? And when I knelt by my bolster as a new Christ follower, I experienced God's presence in a way that delivered peace strengthened by his grace, reinforced by his Word, encouraged by the Spirit, shored up by his promises, supported by his love, and sustained by his provision. Bolstered peace!

Pillowcase Peace

As an adult, I have a new pillowcase tradition.

If only pillows could solve our problems—they are certainly familiar with them. During the day, my busyness is a good distraction, but when I slow down at bedtime, my concerns, trials, and regrets all catch up with me. I try to live with intention to prevent having regrets. But sometimes, as I try to fall asleep, my natural bent is to focus on the negatives of the day. I call that mental activity my

pillowcase regrets. If I allow it to continue, I keep replaying those thoughts. Rehearsing wounds and what-ifs.

I've learned to end the negative thought-reel playing in my head by visualizing a stop sign. It takes the discipline of thought-stopping to prevent a night of tossing and turning in bed. I swap destructive thoughts for God thoughts. Rather than focusing on what I regret or the painful wounds from others' words, I listen for God's still small voice through his Spirit. He reinforces what his Word says and helps me have a better perspective.

> End the negative thought-reel playing in your head by visualizing a stop sign.

If sleep still can't find me, I rehearse the blessings of the day. I thank God for specific gifts and acknowledge that every good gift comes from him. I practice the "think on these things" list (see below). What do I get? No more pillowcase regrets. Instead—pillowcase peace!

Philippians 4:8–9

> *Fix your thoughts on what is true, and honorable, and right, and pure, and lovely, and admirable. Think about things that are excellent and worthy of praise. Keep putting into practice all you learned and received from me—everything you heard from me and saw me doing. Then the God of peace will be with you.*

- What are the verb phrases in this passage? These are our marching orders.
- What are the nouns in this passage? These are our thought targets.
- What is the result of doing this exercise?

When the God of peace is with you, you are more likely to rest in the sweet sleep of peace.

Tag, You're It

Playing tag as kids, we shouted, "Olly olly oxen free!" (What does that mean, anyway?). I always ran toward our "safe" place, but there was a risk that one of the ornery boys in my neighborhood would push me off of base and try to tag me anyway. That's sort of like what pensive peace is. I know I'm safe, but there are things others can do that might mess up that peace.

> When the God of peace is with you, you are more likely to rest in the sweet sleep of peace.

To me, I guess *pensive peace* means I'm at peace, but I also know how my life has been going. I manage my expectations so I don't get hurt again. I trust that God is with me in whatever my current situation is. Because of this, I don't doubt him.

Pensive peace means I know God will take care of me in this matter, and that gives me peace. But the fear of the unknown causes me pensiveness—hesitancy—wondering what I will have to endure before this is resolved. Pensive peace leads me to pray like Jesus. Let this cup pass from me, but even so, Lord, your will be done.*

Have you ever had a closed door to something you thought for sure would be the right direction, only to have an out-of-this-world peace that all is for the best? Not a happy-go-lucky, tra-la-la peace, but an inner voice reassuring you that the right open door will be such an incredible opportunity that it will be worth the wait. We often get frustrated when the door we want to open remains closed, but we forget to see that God has a bigger picture view than we do. He might be working out all the details while we wait. And then, of course, the actions of others can either help or hurt an outcome. While we wait, God gives us bolstered peace so we have some hope to hang on to.

---

* Matthew 26:36–46

Psalm 4:8

> *In peace I will lie down and sleep, for you alone, O Lord, will keep me safe.*

Proverbs 12:20

> *Joy fills hearts that are planning peace!*

Colossians 3:15

> *And let the peace that comes from Christ rule in your hearts. For as members of one body you are called to live in peace. And always be thankful.*

During the PAUSE

Pray

Father, thank you for trading out my pensive peace for your amazing, bolstered peace. Help me block out the intruders that threaten my reception of your peace.

Adjust

I will focus on God's peace whenever my fears and doubts attempt to take over.

Undertake

I will create a visual diversion (such as a stop sign) when I need to stop my thoughts. Instead of being overwhelmed by uncertainties, I will concentrate on the certainties of God's Word.

Seek

I will search for elusive peace when my mind and heart won't shut off.

Evaluate

I will assess my peace levels. If I'm running on low, I'll get a fill-up based on a ready supply of hope.

QUOTE: "[The] lull is a comma, not a period. It's a gift of time from a loving God. I can use it to rethink priorities, set . . . goals, hone new skills. Persistence urges me into action and hope marches up my spine. I shiver with delight. Yes, there is hope in the waiting." –Dianne Christner[29]

ME in the RAW: How am I supposed to be at peace when I'm stuck in this rut? Sure, I know it's not permanent, but it's lasting longer than I can manage on my own.

ME in the SPIRIT: Lord, if you are at the end of my wait, I will wait for you. And if your presence will be my peace during this lull, I will learn to be content— and even find my hope again.

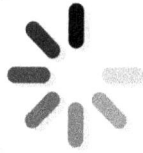

Chapter Nineteen

HELD BY GOD WHEN LIFE'S ON HOLD

When we're stuck in the middle of a trial or a test, waiting for the way out, we crave comfort. It is then that God holds us in his big strong arms. He supports us, he soothes us, he sustains us. What can we do to sense that comfort more? Often, it isn't so much about *what* we're holding on to; it's about *who* is holding us that matters during this time on hold.

Daddy's Arms

One of my favorite memories of childhood was being held by my daddy. Was there someone caring and strong in your early life you can call to memory when thinking about God holding you? When I was wee-bitty, he managed me with ease in one arm (*so strong!*). Then as I grew bigger (and squirmier!), we had a new holding-me routine. As he stood, he let me wrap my legs around his trunk and my arms around his neck. When Mom wasn't looking (although I'm sure she was because she saw *everything*), I'd sit up on his shoulders, even. This was one of my favorite hangout spots when we were outdoors. Like having a human treehouse.

I sat on my daddy's lap in "his" chair until I was almost as tall as him. There was just something about being held by my dad that made me feel like I was safe and secure. I lost him way too early. He was fifty-two, and I was twenty-four. I've spent many more years alive without him than I had him, and that's such a hard thing. But one thing I've learned is that my heavenly Father still holds me and assures me all is well.

It's been amazing to experience something similar all this time I've been fighting chronic diseases. I've had this very real perception that God is holding me, much like the safe and secure love I felt from my earthly father when he held me. I've sensed it over and over and over again.

> *But Lord, be merciful to us, for we have waited for you. Be our strong arm each day and our salvation in times of trouble.*
>
> (Isaiah 33:2)

Your Life Verse

A church friend made me a religious plaque. (I don't normally love those, so I barely paid attention to it, I admit.) Then one day after coming home from the extended hospital stay I described in the last chapter, God led me to really *look* at it. The gift's creator had apologized for not knowing my life verse. He said he normally asks the recipient their favorite verse before making the knick-knack. But since he didn't know mine, he just picked a verse—he wasn't even sure why he selected it. I figured it would be random.

> My heavenly Father holds me and assures me all is well.

I felt a nudge from God to *look* at it. It says, "Don't be afraid or discouraged. I will strengthen you and help you. I will hold you up, for I am your God." This was an abbreviated version of Isaiah 41:10. Wow. God will hold me up. That's exactly what he's been doing. It is especially meaningful when I have setbacks and feel my progress is more like two steps forward, three steps back. What a comfort to know God holds me during these temporary waiting periods. Because I get to be with him, I no longer feel on hold.

I've also witnessed God's incredible protective power in about the biggest way I've ever personally experienced. After the hospitalization when I had sepsis, I received my hospital records. Eye-opening. They contained a long list of pretty awful things wrong with me—most of them the doctors never mentioned to me. That's how I found out I had sepsis,

> There are different miracles. God hasn't chosen to heal me. But I still experience miracles taking place within the brokenness.

along with respiratory failure and a partially collapsed lung caused by a large mucous plug, and more. They identified a rare mix of bacteria. And about twenty other findings. One thing about it was reading that at least helped me not feel wimpy for taking so long to recover. But mostly, it caused me to say aloud, "Thank you, Father." He looked out for me when I was at my worst. At the time, I had a very real sense that I was deathly sick but that it was going to be okay.

There are different miracles. God hasn't chosen to heal me. But I still experience miracles taking place within the brokenness. In that instance, he spared my life and slowed me down so I could know his presence was enough to get me through a difficult time. I don't mean to sound melodramatic, but I also don't want to miss a chance to give God glory for what he did in my life.

I shared that example with my niece Jessica. She wrote me back and said, "I wanted to let you know that something you said in your email with your health updates really touched my heart. You said, 'There are different miracles,' and that was such a great reminder to me. So often, I think I know how God should work and how things should go when I really just need to let

God work the miracles *he* wants to work in *his* time. Your words are going to stay with me a long time. They'll be something I really try to remember when I get discouraged that things aren't going how I think they should go."

Homesick

When we're stuck in the middle of a pause, it stirs up a craving for a real relationship with the Father and makes us homesick. The definition of homesick is "longing for home and family while absent from them."[30]

This reminds me of a song by Squire Parsons that Russ and I used to sing called "Sweet Beulah Land." A recording of us singing it was played at my father's funeral. Just hearing the opening notes of it makes me melancholy all over again.

> When life is hard and the wait is long, heaven sounds sweeter, and being with God means more to us.

When life is going well, we're oftentimes too filled up with present goodness to miss God or long for heaven. But when life is hard, and the wait is long, heaven sounds sweeter, and being with God means more to us.

God's Nature

God knows what we're going through and the ultimate outcome. He's not surprised by the emotions we experience during the wait. He gives us this time to overcome any inaccurate perceptions we might have so we can adjust to what is true. God can see the future now, and because of that, we can trust his timing. Jesus's prayer at Gethsemane shows us how we can trust God despite how we feel. The humanity inside him struggled, yet he did not sin because he trusted his Father to know what was best. And Jesus knew it was best too.[*]

---

[*]   Matthew 26:36–46

During the PAUSE

Pray

Father, help me find peace in being held in your competent, strong arms. Cure my homesickness for you even if you decide not to give me the miracle I seek.

Adjust

I will trade my weakness for your strength.

Undertake

I will slow down enough to cherish being held by you rather than feeling held up in my plans.

Seek

I will sense the comfort of your presence when I'm feeling discontented.

Evaluate

I will evaluate where I'm seeking my comfort. It's not in food or folly but in a Father.

QUOTE: "Even on our hardest days, in our darkest moments, the Lord who knows us meets us. His hand grabs hold of us and doesn't let go." –Katie Faris[31]

ME in the RAW: How is God going to remedy my situation if he's busy holding my hand? I *do* want him to hold me close! But I want him to go and fix the problem. I don't know what I want!

ME in the SPIRIT: What a comfort to know my God is big enough to hold on to me and to be busy about the work at the same time.

Chapter Twenty

WISH UPON A STAR

Have you noticed that wishing your problems away doesn't work? What can we do when there's nothing we can do? We can recognize the techniques that don't work and avoid them. Then we start to learn how to be content while we wait. Praying turns wishes into conversations with God. Changing wishes to prayers trades the power of the universe for the power of the One who created the universe.

Wishing Games

Growing up, I was a good wisher. I believed in the power of a good wish. Perhaps children experience the faith of wishing as a warm-up exercise for learning to place their faith in God through prayer. All I know is I played all the wishing games.

- See a wishing well (or fountain)? Drop in a penny.
- Birthday candles? Blow them out.
- Turkey wishbone (otherwise known as a pully bone)? Get the long end.
- Necklace clasp in front? Wish as you place it behind your neck.

- First star? Wish away! "Star light, star bright / First star I see tonight / I wish I may, I wish I might / Have the wish I wish tonight."

A four-leaf clover was a little harder to find, but I managed it. It made for a special day. Rainbows gave me the same thrill. But I never did find a genie in a bottle.

Then, there were the dandelions. I'm so thankful Mom let me blow on fuzzy dandelions to make wishes as a child. I recently learned that some moms don't allow their children to blow dandelion wishes because the spreading of seeds makes for more dandelion babies to weed later. My mom let me live in the present. And *that* was a present.

My White Knight

A junior in high school, I landed the role of Marian the Librarian in the musical *The Music Man.* The highlight of the casting was that my boyfriend, Rusty, got the part of Harold Hill. He was my real-life Music Man. I got to sing several dreamy romantic songs in the play. Later in the performance, we sang the mushiest song. We crooned "Till There Was You" hand-in-hand on the footbridge with a thirteen-measure kiss thrown in (almost an entire minute). I was the first girl Russ ever kissed, so this on-stage smooch in front of our parents, our pastor, and God made me blush, flush, and everyone else hush!

> Contentment is the capability to be at peace when all else is at war.

In another song, I sang "Goodnight My Someone" as I looked out upon the stars and hoped love would enter my dreams. But there was another song in the musical that was extra special, "My White Knight." In this scene, I imagined what I dreamed of in a man. I wished for the kind of white knight who would love me more than he loved himself and love us even more than me.

The romance didn't end at the conclusion of the play. A year later, my white knight gave me an engagement ring. A year after that, we were married and going to college. My wishes and dreams came true.

When Wishing Doesn't Work

In my childhood, I mastered wishing, but it took growing up to learn some things more important than wishes—like contentment and prayer.

> *But godliness actually is a source of great gain when accompanied by contentment [that contentment which comes from a sense of inner confidence based on the sufficiency of God].*

(1 Timothy 6:6 AMP)

Contentment is the capability to be at peace when all else is at war. It's being grateful even when you still have a long wish list. How might you grow more contented in your life?

- Release desires for material possessions. Attaining things won't make you content.
- Ask God to give you eyes to see the needs of others, and then give of your own time, talents, and treasures.
- Create a gratitude journal, Thankful Thursday blog, social network gratitude updates, etc. (I call mine *grateful gratitudes*.)
- Swap for a better attitude when anything resembling discontentment enters your mind.
- Overcome your fears by focusing on God's power and presence.
- Stay confident in the direction you are going when you know it's the way God is leading.
- Trust God when you can't trust yourself or others.

Ask yourself—how do each of these steps look today when I put them on? Create specific action steps. When you don't base your actions on your feelings, your attitudes will shift to more contentment and less unhappiness and restlessness.

Prayer is the communication of a needy child to a Father who can supply all needs. It's talking to God about even your wants rather than making empty wishes. Knowing God owns the cattle on a thousand hills and the money to pay my bills—he has all I need and want within his power.* But it's more than merely what God has that can help my situation. It's about who he is that can help me the most—and when I talk with him in everyday conversation, prayer provides a way to sense his nearness and his *God-ness*.

> I'm learning not to dwell in the land of jealousy or regrets. I don't like the amenities of their hotels!

How to be more prayerful in your life? Talk to God when you are:

- **Confused.** He will give you wisdom and discernment.
- **Worried.** He will calm your fears.
- **Needy.** He will provide for your needs or be all you need.
- **Happy.** He will rejoice with you. (Perhaps thunder is God's happy dance when he celebrates our good times with us!)
- **Busy.** He will help you pace your day.
- **Restless.** He will give you stability.
- **Suffering.** He will sustain you.

If Only . . .

> *And don't be wishing you were someplace else or with someone else. Where you are right now is God's place for you. Live and obey and love and believe right there.*
>
> (1 Corinthians 7:17 MSG)

---

* Psalm 50:10

156

When I feel overwhelmed and start comparing my life with others, I can easily believe I'm somehow "less than." I'm learning not to dwell in the land of jealousy or regrets. I don't like the amenities of their hotels!

Sometimes I catch myself wishing for what someone else has (a belonging, a job, health, a relationship, etc.). It must be a common human trait because it's mentioned in several ways in the Ten Commandments. I've learned to pray about it and ask God to help me be content in what I have—pleased that others have something I only wish for—and for direction if I'm supposed to pursue something I don't have.

I ask God to give me a burning passion if it's something he wants to instigate in my life. And I ask God to give me *heartburn* if it's a no-go. (Not literal heartburn, obviously, but that internal sense that it isn't right.) Take it off the list if it isn't a God-dream. I can't expect him to equip me with the wherewithal to complete something if it's not in his plan for my life. Rather than having a comparison list or a jealousy list, I have a prayer list. A very *specific* prayer list. If God wants to make it happen, it's up to him to bring it to pass. My part is to be willing and to risk dreaming big with God.

> I will trade out my wish list for God's will.

One big caveat on this dreaming big thing is to not get caught up in comparing ourselves with others. The Bible says it's not wise to do that. God made us different for a *reason*. It's crazy-making to think we can have someone else's life. Instead, God wants to create an individualized, unique, goal list that is customized, tailor-made to fit each of us. My list is only for *me*. Your list is only for *you*. In order for that to work, I have to ask God to show me some crazy big things he has just for me. I can't look over at your list to grab all the good ideas. God isn't a copycat God. He gives me some original ideas that are *just for me*—if I seek them.

It's time to put on my thinking cap and ask God to show me what dream-big ideas he has for me. It's my grown-up wish list. And in the meantime, learning to be content is at the top.

During the PAUSE

Pray

Father, I want to be more content than I am right now. I know it represents having a joy-filled peace that only comes from you. Only I'm not feeling so joyful or peaceful. I've been guilty of wishing my way out of this mess rather than being content right here, right now. Help!

Adjust

I will trade out my wish list for your will.

Undertake

I will make a list of my wishes for something different than this. For each one, I'll come up with a way to be content with what is going on (or the absence of anything going on) right now.

Seek

I will discover a new way to adopt a contented mindset to make this my new default.

Evaluate

I will evaluate what techniques I've attempted before that didn't help me learn to be more content.

QUOTE: "Contentment is a settled spirit, quiet confidence that God is always at work for good." –Melissa Kruger[32]

ME in the RAW: But if I don't have a settled spirit, how can I find contentment? I don't have confidence in anything right now—just confusion!

ME in the SPIRIT: I will take all my wishes and even my whining and have a little chat with Jesus until he settles me down and brings peace to my heart.

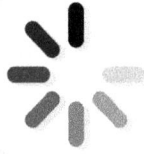

Chapter Twenty-One

THE BEGINNING OF GRAND ADVENTURES

Sometimes we can't change the delay, but we can change the way we look at it. We don't have to wait until the lull is over to get to the good stuff. Let's find (or create) some fun along the way. When we begin to realize that God equips us for grand adventures that happen *during* on-hold seasons, we can learn not to hate the wait. It might seem as if nothing is productive or effective during this pause, but it can accomplish great God-things in our lives and the lives of others who watch us wait.

Stuck on the Elevator

I've been thinking about waiting and delays. This is what I've decided: delays are the beginning of grand adventures. Don't clutter the journey with wondering what-ifs when you could be experiencing a new kind of faith. And when I say *you*, I mean me too!

Our deadlines are not God's timetable. When we yield our agenda to God's purpose, we can anticipate goodness is on the way. It's like my parents' coffeepot from years gone by. When they heard it percolating, they knew the end result was worth the wait. It's rather sad how we rush the coffee process these days—and the life process, for that matter. Face it, our agenda is based on selfish desires and prideful perceptions that we think we know best what the schedule should be. Waiting isn't as painful when we can anticipate great things ahead. But often, these delays make us feel stuck.

> Don't clutter the journey with wondering what-ifs when you could be experiencing a new kind of faith!

Waiting without listening to God is like sitting down at a restaurant table and waiting for the waitress without looking at the menu. How will you know what to expect?

How do you know if you're stuck? It's when your life feels like an elevator that's stopped between floors. What can you do when it happens? Much like the passengers in the elevator, it's about learning that God's presence is enough. If not, you will focus so much on the problem, you'll panic. Rationally, you know it's a temporary nuisance when compared to the fullness of life. Still, in the moment, it feels restrictive. Someone else is running the show, and there's nothing you can do about it. Aha! That's the problem. It's a matter of losing control in the wait. It's also about learning contentment, especially as I see others getting ahead.

Jealousy

When I feel stuck, it's easy to get jealous of others living my dream life. I'm happy for them, but I'm disappointed that I'm not the main character in the dream scene. Being content with now is key.

It seems like I've done everything right to get to the outcome someone else is living out. I surrendered my life to God for his use. I made sacrifices to stay focused. I yielded my bad attitudes and learned God-like characteristics.

I made sure to kick my personal agendas to the curb and sign up for God-led goals. I killed my ego, crucified my pride, to make sure anything I set out to do was for God, by God, through God, not *Kathy*. So, why this current roadblock?

True confession—being on hold feels like punishment when I'm so eager to live out the life God inserted into my dreams. As I pray for discernment, I don't sense God's Spirit using this wait to discipline or penalize me for something I've done. I'm happy others are getting to be productive right now, but when does *my* "right now" come?

I'm ashamed to admit this. I don't want to feel jealous. And I'm mostly able to be content. But there are times, especially when I'm worn down and tired, that I grow impatient. During these moments of weakness is when I notice others are advancing while I'm standing still. I don't want to be jealous. Being honest about these pangs of envy is uncomfortable. It's such an ugly emotion. As I confess it, I ask God to create in me a clean and pure heart again (and again). One that's just as joy-filled when I'm *being* as when I'm *doing*.

God has purpose in the wait, too!

I don't have to fill a bio or have a bottomless to-do list to be significant to God. And I don't have to always be chasing a dream or a goal to live out the purpose God has in my life. I can put this jealousy to death only when I'm truly content smack dab in the middle of this holding pattern.

I'm not jealous of their fame, their possessions, or even their abilities. I'm jealous because I want the same opportunities to serve God. Is that so wrong?

It helps to know that God doesn't withhold any good thing from me. Whatever he brings my way is customized to fit me for the most joy.

> *Even strong young lions sometimes go hungry, but those who trust in the Lord will lack no good thing.*
>
> (Psalm 34:10)

> *For the Lord God is our sun and our shield. He gives us grace and glory. The Lord will withhold no good thing from those who do what is right.*
>
> (Psalm 84:11)

Whatever God permits in my life will bring him big glory if I don't get in the way.

The Fruit of the Wait

I certainly didn't expect to be where I am at this point in my life. I honestly thought I would experience the actualization of the goals I thought God had placed in my heart. Instead, I've had enough roadblocks to know I can't wait for the goals to come true to live out God's purpose in my life.

I'm using these pauses to inhale and exhale in the breathing pattern of experiencing God in this moment. As I do that, I'm learning how to flourish during the *wait*. That's so much better than postponing the enjoyment of my life for when I get to live out what I perceived to be God's design in me. What I'm learning is that

> I will use this wait to focus on how my circumstance could actually be used to encourage someone else.

God has a purpose in the *wait* too. What feels like an unproductive season may produce the most important fruit of all.

Here's where it gets real. Even if I have good intentions, if I'm unhappy that I'm stuck rather than in go-gear, then I'm missing out on God's best for my life. And the root problem is that I've spent too much time focusing on self. I need to stop looking at the lives of others and wishing for that. Instead of saying, "But God, I wanted to sing that song. I wanted to get that invitation. I deserved that promotion. I longed for ____," I need to stop fussing over it. Even if the intention is good, if it's a self-focus, then it's not a God-focus, is it? See how we get it all confused and start taking the spotlight off the One who truly matters? We trade the object of our priorities (a God focus) for self-focused priorities. Then we trade those for what hinders us, and before we know it, we have spiraled into a very messy spot.

Ways to get out of the mess:

- Stop worrying about self all the time.
- Find a way to be a blessing to someone else.
- Give God back your agenda, your goals, and your dreams.

During the PAUSE

Pray

Father, I invite you into this wait with me to show me how to be content and to even thrive while I wait for something to change.

Adjust

I will swap out my impatience for peace, my jealousy for contentment.

Undertake

I will use this wait to focus on how my circumstance could actually be used to encourage someone else.

Seek

I will seek God's will and embrace it, even if it means abandoning an expectation for accomplishment.

Evaluate

I will determine if I'm willing to wait and trust or if my motives are self-serving.

QUOTE: "When we face these frustrating delays, we automatically assume that He is denying us, neglecting us or rejecting us. So we throw a childish pity party. We go in our rooms, close our doors, shut out the pain and stay as far away from Jesus as possible." –J. Lee Grady[33]

ME in the RAW: Delays are no fun because they deny me the very things I've worked hard to achieve!

ME in the SPIRIT: My childish antics restrict me from enjoying the fruit of this delay. I need to grow up and not just face the music but dance during the wait!

Chapter Twenty-Two

IT'S NOT ABOUT THE FIX BUT THE FUTURE

Anyone who has ever dealt with a trial or challenge in life knows what it's like to have someone else try to fix you or fix your problem. When that happens, it's easy to feel misunderstood—or perhaps even feel like a burden to civilization. Consider new ways to endure the wait that leads to a hope-filled future, even when others are off base in how they attempt to rescue you from your mess. When we feel broken, the best fix is to find our wholeness in Christ. He is the Master Fixer-Upper.

> *So spacious is he, so expansive, that everything of God finds its proper place in him without crowding. Not only that, but all the broken and dislocated pieces of the universe—people and things, animals and atoms—get properly fixed and fit together in vibrant harmonies, all because of his death, his blood that poured down from the cross.*
>
> (Colossians 1:19–20 MSG)

Why Others Try to Fix Us

People love to fix the brokenness they see in other people. I'm guilty of this flaw myself. I try to fix things in other people even when they don't ask for my help. When someone is struggling, rather than sitting by and simply listening, or praying, or learning more about his or her issues, I jump in, trying to make something better for them. Or worse, I help them identify why they are in the mess, to begin with.

My goodness—I sound like one of Job's friends! Job in the Bible had multiple plights happening one after another. The most helpful thing his friends did was to take time to show up and to quietly sit with Job in his sufferings. Until they opened their mouths. That was when they began to be unhelpful. In their minds, they thought they could fix him. I've been guilty of this. And others have certainly tried to fix me too.

> My heart's desire and good intention is to simply come alongside someone without giving unsolicited advice.

Why do we do this whole fixing thing? And when is it okay? A significant factor in this scenario is how well the "fixer" knows the "broken one." Only someone invested in my everyday life has the right to butt in when they see something that can use improvement. Strangers and acquaintances haven't earned that right. If we aren't familiar enough with a person, we can so easily misunderstand them, assume the wrong things, jump to conclusions, and say the wrong things. All it manages to do is injure the relationship.

I do try to give the benefit of the doubt to the fixer and look at their heart intentions. Often, they don't know me well enough and end up saying something "helpful" that is *so* off-target. Of course, we have to leave room for the Lord to work in and through people too. I'm not discrediting that. But I think we rush in to rescue someone way too fast. We don't even have time to put on our superhero capes! We jump in so quickly, thinking we have all the answers. Often, there are questions that don't need to be answered right away. It's in the wait that we grow.

I'm learning to do less fixing. My heart's desire and good intention is to simply come alongside someone without giving unsolicited advice. Instead, I desire to give them unconditional love and be available to wait it out with them. (But I admit this is a work in progress.)

Motives for Fixers

People have different motives for trying to improve someone's situation:

- We want to make them feel better so we'll feel better, or at least we want to feel good that we tried to help—we make it about us.

- We think we have an answer they haven't considered. Surely, we have special knowledge they are missing.

- We can't fix something about ourselves, but when we see the same challenge or flaw in someone else, we can easily point it out to them.

- We really do care, and because it's so torturous to sit in the waiting room of life with them, we try to hurry up their wait by giving them answers for which they haven't asked.

- Their trial has caused us to revisit a similar trial we had in our own life. We have accumulated wisdom

> Humility partners well when helping someone stuck in getting out of the hole.

based on that experience and want to share it. But we forget that perhaps the one in the waiting room right now also has previous experience to help them through this. God equips us with what we need. Sometimes it's through a person he leads to help, and sometimes through prior life lessons.

How easy it is for us! We intrude in their private space. We say, "Maybe it's *this*, or maybe it's *that*. Have you tried . . . ?" We think it's okay to butt in. Even if they respond guardedly, we push harder, thinking we have the solution if they would just listen.

There are times when others try to fix me that they start meddling in a way that feels a lot like personal accusations. They need me to know it's my fault I'm in this dilemma—on hold—not hearing from God. If I had more faith, or took more action, or made better decisions, or chose better solutions, I would not be in this pickle. Or, if only I had listened to them, I wouldn't be in this mess. People just love playing the savior!

> It's never appropriate to pile guilt on someone who is hurting.

I should clarify—the primary time it bugs me when someone tries to fix me is when they hardly know me. They are so off the mark in their help that I feel misunderstood. That adds to my level of frustration rather than alleviating pressure. Definitely, when someone is the voice of reason, even if I barely know them, even if it ruffles my feathers at first, I will take what they have given me as a dose of good medicine. But it sure is nice to help it go down with a little bit of sugar rather than them sounding superior in some way. Humility partners well when helping someone stuck in getting out of the hole.

There are times I receive good wisdom from others, and I don't buck against their advice. I recognize it's good for me, and their motives are for my good. But if someone rubs me the wrong way with the wrong sort of help at the wrong time, then I'm rubbed raw. I call them sandpaper people because their grit causes me to grit my teeth!

I've learned from personal experience that when I offer someone in a holding pattern a remedy, it needs to always be accompanied by some soothing balm. What can I do to help? How might my words hurt? What a difference it will make if I ask those questions before I open my mouth (or post that comment or email that note).

Maybe you don't identify as a fixer. But I'm guessing no one gets through life without encountering someone who tries to fix them.

Offering Comfort or Compassion

How can we offer comfort or compassion instead of solutions? During a recent on-hold experience, the ones who ministered to me the most were the ones who acknowledged how yucky the situation was without having to attach a solution to the problem. One even said, "I have no words—I'm so sorry—this really is poopy."

Don't get me wrong. Sometimes God does want us to participate in their way out. But when we hurry to fix them, do we ask God first if it's the right time, if it's the right answer, or if we're the right ones to help? Or do we rush in to rescue them—moving so fast we almost forget that superhero cape?

As God leads, yes, we can help. We'll know when it's time. The broken one might even reach out to us and ask for help. That's a pretty good cue to proceed. Perhaps then we can break it down and evaluate the different parts of what is stinky and what to do next.

When we do it right, it doesn't sound like we're preaching at them or pointing a finger of blame. Even though I love hearing sermons in church and reading sermons, I don't much care for getting a sermon disguised as concerned advice. It leaves me feeling that if I did something different, this wouldn't keep happening to me. And yes, there are times I wonder that myself, but I wouldn't say that to someone else. It's never appropriate to pile guilt on someone who is hurting.

We don't make it through life without being distressed, but the true peace we can have comes from Jesus because of his completed mission to restore us. This is where we find courageous joy, and it's the only fix we can offer others.

> *"I have told you these things, so that in Me you may*
> *have [perfect] peace. In the world you have tribulation*

and distress and suffering, but be courageous [be confident, be undaunted, be filled with joy]; I have overcome the world." [My conquest is accomplished, My victory abiding.]

(John 16:33 AMP)

Don't Try to Fix Me!

As you've probably figured out by now in this chapter, I have little tolerance for someone misunderstanding me and then trying to remedy a perceived wrong. Does it bug you when others try to "fix" something about you? Do you feel as if they are butting into your life (even though they mean well)?

Sometimes someone says they are praying that I don't get discouraged and gives me tips for not becoming discouraged. Perhaps their default setting is discouragement, so when they read my news, they assume I'm discouraged. That's not usually the place in my mind where I tend to hang out. When I receive warnings not to get discouraged, I feel like they don't know me well. I'm not really "wired" to feel defeated or depressed. If I were, it would have happened years ago. I have plenty of other weak links, though.

> I will dig deep to see what is truly bothering me when someone gives me advice.

I do get frustrated with human error, and I dislike being misunderstood, but there's something deeper than those emotions that gives me a good amount of stick-to-it-ness and even joy. It's a gift from God to be able to have that sort of frame of mind and heart, and I don't take it lightly. Or maybe I'm just stubborn and don't let disappointing news discourage me. If anything, I see it as God narrowing my options so I can choose something different with greater ease. Bad news is one way we gain wisdom that leads us toward good news. (And I'm so glad for that because I can use a-lotta-lotta wisdom!)

We can't make it out of our holding patterns without other people trying to fix us. It feels like they are pouring salt on our wounds. But their motives often come from a good place. They simply misunderstand because they assume upon us the emotion they would feel if they were the one in our shoes.

During the PAUSE

Pray

Father, help me be open-minded to your fixes. And give me discernment for the best response to fixes from others. I don't want to miss your wisdom simply because I'm resistant to their advice.

Adjust

I will learn to be less riled up when others give me unsolicited advice by seeing they care.

Undertake

I will focus on the nugget of truth buried in the remedies from know-it-alls.

Seek

I will dig deep to see what is truly bothering me when someone gives me advice.

Evaluate

I will check myself to see if I'm annoying others by sending them unwelcome suggestions.

QUOTE: "Brokenness to redemption, where mercy and grace kiss both sides of our face.

Brokenness where we are split open.

Redemption where God knits us back together.

Mercy when we don't get the punishment we do deserve.

Grace when we get the lavish love gifts we don't deserve.

So here we are." –Lysa TerKeurst[34]

ME in the RAW: So now I'm not merely waiting, stuck in making progress—I'm also broken? Oh great! Now we have to go on a self-improvement kick before I even get to enjoy something other than this broken record.

ME in the SPIRIT: I come to the Father broken, knowing he will repair what ails me. It's not up to me to fix myself but to receive the medicine from the Physician.

Chapter Twenty-Three

RELIEF ISN'T IN RESULTS BUT IN RETREAT

E ven though we tend to resist when others try to fix us, we go to great lengths to try to fix ourselves or resolve our circumstances. We'd do just about anything to reverse being on hold. Often, it's less about what we need to do and more about where we need to go to find relief. Learning to retreat helps us not only get out of the holding pattern but also helps us be content and joy-filled as we wait.

I've had several incredible personal retreats in my life. Each one seemingly orchestrated by God himself, who was the host waiting for me when I arrived. Some of them lasted mere hours—at a café with Wi-Fi. Others lasted days at an away location or even a retreat center. Some retreats are as simple as going out to my porch swing, away from the distractions of television, internet, and phone.

What if we looked at the word retreat as re-"treat"? Retreats are an opportunity to give ourselves something wonderful?[35]

> *Then Jesus said, "Let's go off by ourselves to a quiet place and rest awhile." He said this because there were so many people coming and going that Jesus and his apostles didn't even have time to eat.*
>
> (Mark 6:31)

The Month of Wow

Here's a piece I wrote while on a personal retreat at Arrowhead Bible Camp in Wisconsin after having fourteen speaking programs in about as many days. I understood why Jesus wanted to get away after meeting with the multitudes. When I wrapped up speaking for a women's retreat as my final gig, I enjoyed an extra two-day stay in their cottage for God-and-me time.

I wrote:

> God has shown up in so many beautiful ways, and today he's put the bow on the package. My heart felt the Spirit say, "Sweet child, here you go—just for you."
>
> My time has been jam-packed with blessings and affirmations. I see my Father everywhere I look. In the pastoral countryside, the graces of individuals, the heart connections. God is breathing fresh life into me, restoring my soul in supernatural ways.
>
> I came to minister to others and also set aside time to ask God a list of questions regarding decisions for future work and ministry—yes, I had a physical list. I wrote out the meditational thoughts that came to me during the retreat's discipline of silence. The Lord very clearly impressed upon me to put the questions aside and simply enjoy his presence, focus on who he is, and by doing that, I'd be so close to his heartbeat, I'd know the answers to the questions. So, I've been listening to amazing music, walking in his nature, taking photos of his glory expressed in creation, journaling praise and worship, and guess what? Every question now has a tailor-made answer.
>
> These last two days I've been on a personal retreat, alone in a cottage situated on Chain Lake. I awoke with such gratitude—he has drenched me in so many God-things. I'm so very thankful for God's provision after being in a holding pattern for what seemed like eternity.

Grateful for:

- Friends who are more like sisters.
- The support of others who get me and what I'm so passionate to do in my life.
- The brilliance of autumn, which has already shown up with the crisp air and leaves.
- The shimmery glisten of the morning sun on this silvery lake.
- Getting to do what I love most, communicating through spoken and written word in ways that gives others aha! moments that free them from whatever holds them back. What a blessing to know those illuminating inspirations equipped them to move into the glorious role God dreamed up just for them.
- Fourteen speaking programs in just one month. Power-packed. Affirming how incredible this calling is in making a difference—not merely impacting the hearer, but *me*.

My cup, once dry, is full to overflowing, and now I can pour into others from the saucer rather than being emptied of the supply God means solely for me.

That's what happened at one of my retreats. What can happen if you slow down and spend some dedicated time with God alone?

Plan Your Retreat

Let your mind dream about the retreat to fill your empty cup. Where will you go? What will you do? How will you come away refreshed and strengthened to either wait some more, or move forward, depending on God's direction?

Many of my personal retreats include a time for goal setting. Goals help me get unstuck. They make me feel like I'm making progress on what I *do* have control over while I wait for something to change that I *don't* have control over.

177

One great resource for retreating is *Getaway with God: The Everywoman's Guide to Personal Retreat* by Letitia Suk. In the beginning, she writes a letter to the reader called "Dear Friend." She states, "Getting away with God on a personal retreat works like that overnight charge [for our phones]. We plug into the source of all life and let him fill us to the brim. One full charge can last a long time as we resume the race set before us. Hope returns, peace floods in, and the mental fog lifts. Something about hanging out with the creator of the universe brings things into perspective."[36]

> ▶ Put the questions aside and simply enjoy God's presence.

When I think of having God-and-me time during a spiritual retreat, I am reminded of Psalm 23. As a child, I memorized it in the King James Version, and that still comes to mind. If you haven't read it in that translation, I recommend you do so to prepare your heart for the refreshing time of retreating. But for a different perspective on the classic, I'm sharing it in *The Message* paraphrase here.

> *God, my shepherd!*
>   *I don't need a thing.*
> *You have bedded me down in lush meadows,*
>   *you find me quiet pools to drink from.*
> *True to your word,*
>   *you let me catch my breath*
>   *and send me in the right direction.*
> *Even when the way goes through*
>   *Death Valley,*
> *I'm not afraid*
>   *when you walk at my side.*
> *Your trusty shepherd's crook*
>   *makes me feel secure.*

You serve me a six-course dinner
right in front of my enemies.
You revive my drooping head;
my cup brims with blessing.
Your beauty and love chase after me
every day of my life.
I'm back home in the house of God
for the rest of my life.

(Psalm 23 MSG)

The Rest of the Story

I left a holding pattern when I went on the personal retreat I described above. Then I returned home ready to move forward. I thought for sure I knew what God wanted me to do. But I quickly learned the retreat wasn't meant to get me ready for doing. It was meant to prepare me for another pause. I entered a four-year sabbatical that took me from one medical dilemma to another. This on-hold period included:

> When you feel like you can't wait one more day for your life to change, instead of trying to push forward, advance by retreating.

- A ten-day hospital stay for sepsis and pneumonia
- Three surgeries
- Cancer treatment
- Three rounds of PT with many grueling sessions each round
- New medications, new doctors, new tests, new diagnoses (I lost count!)

At first, I was frustrated for not getting to progress with the goals I thought God led me to set during that retreat. Weary and wary. But then I realized that's why God led me to put away my brainstorming questions during my retreat to spend time with him. His presence was what I needed not only for the retreat, but it was my sustaining grace in the days ahead.

So, when you feel like you can't wait one more day for your life to change, instead of trying to push forward, advance by retreating. God will equip you with what you need, even though you don't know you need it yet.

During the PAUSE

Pray

Oh God, in this time of wanting to move forward, I'm slowing down to hear your voice and spend time with you. Even if I don't get answers, I get more of you. You are enough.

Adjust

I will rein in my nature to be busy and learn not to be uncomfortable in the quiet.

Undertake

I will plan a time away, even if it seems counterproductive.

Seek

I will quit looking for solutions and instead seek a Savior.

Evaluate

I will consider why I'm in such a hurry for progress and productivity.

QUOTE: "'Wait on the Lord' is a constant refrain in the Psalms, and it is a necessary word, for God often keeps us waiting. He is not in such a hurry as we are, and it is not his way to give more light on the future than we need for action in the present, or to guide us more than one step at a time. When in doubt, do nothing, but continue to wait on God. When action is needed, light will come." –J.I. Packer[37]

ME in the RAW: God may not be in a hurry, but how am I to keep up with the rest of this world, spinning without me, while I'm stuck in this delay? I need action now!

ME in the SPIRIT: Even though the world presses me for results, I will wait on the Lord and retreat into his presence, knowing his love is better than anything the world can offer me.

Chapter Twenty-Four

HELP IS ON THE WAY

P art of the distress after an auto accident is the wait to be rescued. It seems like a *forever wait* after calling 9-1-1. Does anyone care? Did the dispatcher really listen and send help? Will you survive this? Seconds seem like minutes, and minutes seem like hours. But then, in the faint distance, you hear the sirens. What a reassuring sound. Help is on the way! And in life, while waiting it out, hang on to the comfort that help is on the way for you too.

Encouraging Words

Don't be afraid. Just stand still and watch the Lord rescue you today (Exodus 14:13). This passage was spoken by Moses to the people to encourage them to look to God to save them from the Egyptians. It was right after their escape, and Pharoah took his chariot and troops to chase after the Israelites. Sandwiched between that description and the miracle of the Red Sea, Moses spoke these words.

Whatever holding pattern you are in right now is the pause between what was (your Egypt) and what is yet to come (your Red Sea). Hold on. Help is on the way!

Samuel then took a large stone and placed it between the towns of Mizpah and Jeshanah. He named it Ebenezer (which means "the stone of help"), for he said, "Up to this point the Lord has helped us!" (1 Samuel 7:12). What Ebenezer stone can we use to remind ourselves that God has helped us before, and he will be our help now and in the future? It can be any tangible reminder of God's assistance and relief—his provision for what we need. I have a literal stone given to me by my friend Lori Garza that I'm designating as my symbolic Ebenezer stone. On one side, it says "Joy," and on the other side is a painted blue flower. The stone offers a tactile moment too. It's so smooth to the touch.

> It's good to remind ourselves where our help comes from, and what his credentials are. God made heaven and earth!

Knowing God provided for me before and that he can do it again is such a comforting thought. Help is on the way!

But God is my helper. The Lord keeps me alive! (Psalm 54:4). How is God your helper? Has he literally saved your life from death? If not that, how has he rescued you from a bad circumstance?

I took my troubles to the Lord; I cried out to him, and he answered my prayer. Rescue me, O Lord (Psalm 120:1–2). Some say it's wrong to say anything negative to the Lord. But this verse shows that we can bring our troubles to the Lord. His shoulders are big enough to carry whatever our burdens weigh. Cry out to the Lord for help, for rescue. Look to him for answers when you only see problems.

I lift up my eyes to the hills. From where does my help come? My help comes from the Lord, who made heaven and earth (Psalm 121:1–2 ESV). I love the wording in Psalm 121 and have heard songs inspired by this passage. It's good to remind ourselves where our help comes from and what his credentials are. He made heaven and earth! (It's almost a "my daddy is stronger than your daddy" type reminder.)

Please, Lord, rescue me! Come quickly, Lord, and help me. (Psalm 40:13) I find I can be impatient and annoyed by problems that aren't solved quickly. I'm not proud of it. But it's comforting to see that David begged to God out of a sense of urgency too!

God is our refuge and strength, always ready to help in times of trouble (Psalm 46:1). When I wait, God is ready to help. While I wait, God is my refuge and strength.

What Helps, What Doesn't?

Almost ten years ago, I posted this to my Facebook timeline. I received support and wise responses. Seeing this again now shows me that we all go through these pauses in our lives. While some of them may eventually lift (sooner or later), it doesn't make us immune from future waiting periods! [38]

Kathy Carlton Willis:

Several of you have asked what I'm learning during this waiting period in my life. As I journal, I've found some aha! moments I'm turning into a book. So, I have a question for you as part of my research—and also to initiate a conversation because I know I'm not the only one going through yet another holding pattern. QUESTION: What glimmer of sunbeam helped you when it seemed the lights had gone out during your life circumstance? And what did another person say or do in hopes of encouraging you that fell flat, even though they meant well?

Kim Anonymous:

What helped me in the holding pattern? Certain songs, sitting on the deck crying my eyes out and then finding peace in Scripture, and red birds. Every hard day brought a red bird to my deck, and I just felt like it was a sign of hope directly from God.

185

Laura Smith:

> Being held by my hubby, who lets me cry or scream while he holds me tight.

Alice V. Roberts Stattman:

> Lights go out at the end of the tunnel many times. God knows our strengths and weaknesses. Rely on *him*. Each morning I pray for what I will face with grace, dignity, and strength. Friends can talk and help out with little things, but the bigger things are in someone else's hand—our Father. Faith, trust, and belief are what get us through.

Ursula Phillips:

> Never say God won't give you more than you can handle. He routinely gives us more than we can handle. That's what forces us to let him handle it for us.

Suzanne Turner:

> For me, in those times, I think it was the amazing ability of God to restore me every morning.

Wendy Hamilton:

> Stop looking at the big picture and think about the next step.

During the PAUSE

Pray

Oh Rescuer, I am hanging on to the hope and comfort of knowing that your help is already dispatched and on the way. Give me aid, even in the wait.

Adjust

I will change my clock and calendar to focus on God's timetable instead of my own.

Undertake

I will get busy doing something during the wait, knowing God's help will come right on time.

Seek

I will search for God's grace to infuse me, knowing he is a first responder when it comes to hearing my alarm.

Evaluate

I will examine if I'm allowing this wait to cause me to feel desperate, and if so, I will meditate on God as my very present help in time of need.[*]

---

[*] Psalm 46:1

QUOTE: "Experiencing God's faithfulness during these difficult times has enabled me to say with certainty, 'God will help you.'" –Lori Hatcher[39]

ME in the RAW: I know help is on the way, but could God turn on the lights and sirens and get here a little faster?

ME in the SPIRIT: Deep down, I know that God will deliver me from this in just the right time, in the way that best works for his plans. Or he'll redeem it from the messes others and I have made that caused the delay.

Chapter Twenty-Five

GOD IS BIGGER THAN THIS

The trouble with delays or feeling like life is on hold is that our circumstances and issues seem to multiply and magnify. All we can focus on is the bigness of our problems. Yet, probably the most assuring truth we can grasp is to realize that God is bigger than any situation, any heartache, any delay, or any trial. He is bigger than whatever *this* looks like. No matter what, he's got this!

My Daddy has Big Muscles!

Growing up, one of the places I felt safest was in my father's arms. (I first told you about this special bond with my dad in chapter 19.) He was a hard worker and had big muscles—not the kind earned in a fitness center but those developed from muscling through tasks. I look back on early photos of us and see that when I was a baby, he carried me almost like a football. He appeared confident that he wouldn't drop me. Why should he worry? He knew he had carried much heavier weights than mine. He was my strong dad—there was no reason to fear.

Well, my heavenly Daddy has big muscles too! And he has lifted burdens way heavier than mine. He has carried me through previous trials, and he will get me through this one. I can rest in his strong arms and be confident that he will take care of me. My God is bigger than my problems!

Who was the person of strength you recall from your childhood? Some of you don't have fond memories of your father, but maybe someone else took on that role for you. It's good when we can anchor our thoughts about how strong our God is, to think of the strong people in our lives. It might be physical strength, or it could be internal fortitude. But if no one you know comes to mind, that's okay too—because either way, God's got this!

> *As for me, I look to the Lord for help. I wait confidently*
> *for God to save me, and my God will certainly hear me.*
> (Micah 7:7)

How Big Is Big?

Last night on the TV show *Survivor*, I saw a giant player pick up not one but two other male survivors. Their feet went off the ground. The smaller survivor—I could understand. But the second man he picked up was a giant in his own right. A bounty hunter. The hulk of a picker-upper is a former NBA player and 6'11". No wonder he dwarfed the other guys!

How *little* my problems are when compared to how *big* my God is.

It made me think of how *little* my problems are compared to how *big* my God is. He's got this! He's so strong he can pick them up two at a time. (I'm glad about that . . . my problems never seem to come alone—they bring a buddy along!)

This Too Shall Pass

My Grandma Mary used to always say, "This too shall pass," when going through a hard time or waiting for an answer to prayer. That always sounded good, and I know it's true. I often have to simplify it to remind myself. *This. Is. Temporary.*

But last night, while praying through my list and looking at all the things on hold or pause or wait, it began to feel like too much. Even when realizing it's temporary. My snarky side came out, and right in the middle of prayer, when my heart heard the words *this too shall pass,* I said aloud, "So do kidney stones, but they're not much fun during the *during!*"

Those kidney stones seem pretty big, doing damage to our insides, but then they pass, and it's hard to believe something so small can cause

> What matters to you matters to God because *you* matter to God!

such immense pain and suffering. After I thought through that illustration, I came to a point of peace again, realizing my problems are like those kidney stones. My God is so big, and those problems are so small when it comes to his capable healing hands. Yet, he has compassion, knowing how big they seem to me at the time. What started out as a snarky struggle ended up in peaceful rest. Grandma had it right. This too shall pass!

Change the Self-Talk

Often, I have to remind myself, "This feels really big right now—overwhelming, even. But my God is bigger than this. No problem is too big for him to shoulder. What matters to me matters to God even when it feels like it doesn't matter to anyone else. He understands me like no other because he made me and has never left my side." What matters to you matters to God because *you* matter to God!

God Can Do It

I was reminded this week just how big our God is. I knew. I just *knew* that God had something around the corner for us. I had guesses as to how he might take care of us and show us a glimpse of his love. But I didn't *really* know. In fact, I had no clue just how powerful God was to change our outcome.

I think what I've experienced can be called *mustard-seed faith.*[*]
I had a little bit of faith. I had faith enough to think mustard-seed-
sized things might happen. But God took my little bit of faith and
honored it by showing me just how BIG he is.

There have been so many different times God has surprised
me with a better-than-hoped-for outcome. This is a good time for
all of us to remember what God has done for us. It never gets old
to count our blessings or make gratitude lists. But let's get specific.
Think about last year's biggest problem.

Have you had a resolution yet?

- How did it turn out?

- What surprised you about the outcome?

- How did you see God at work in you or in your
circumstance?

If you are going through a human-sized problem, surrender it
to God and wait for his God-sized solution. He has ways to make
things "all better," just like my Mom fixed my child-sized problems. She used to kiss my boo-boos and make the pain go away.
God kisses away my problems and makes his grace come to stay.

I've learned not to limit God or put him in a box. Just when
I think I have figured out how he might take care of my burdens, he
surprises me with a different solution. Yet one more time, he has saved
the day that I can write in my memory book.

> God will meet me in my worst-case and make it not best-case but blessed-case.

When I need a reminder of his goodness, I can pull out these memories of provision as a testimony of his ability to take care of me.

Whatever is good and perfect is a gift coming down
to us from God our Father, who created all the lights

---

[*]   Matthew 17:20

*in the heavens. He never changes or casts a shifting
shadow.*

(James 1:17)

*Have you not known? Have you not heard? The Lord is
the everlasting God, the Creator of the ends of the earth.
He does not faint or grow weary; his understanding is
unsearchable.*

(Isaiah 40:28 ESV)

*When I look at the night sky and see the work of your
fingers—the moon and the stars you set in place—
what are mere mortals that you should think about
them, human beings that you should care for them?*

(Psalm 8:3–4)

Secret to Coping

Someone asked how to cope when overwhelmed by a frightening
circumstance or trial. For me, it always works to ask myself,
"What's the worst thing that ever happened?" Then I remind
myself that *this* isn't worse than *that*. And God was big enough
then, so it stands to reason that he's got this! For example, when
I'm in pain, I remind myself of the crippling couple of years with
complex regional pain syndrome. My body was trying to reject my
foot—acting as if it was the enemy. I made it through that and
am no longer in a wheelchair. There may come a day when I'm in
a wheelchair to stay, but no matter the circumstance, I'm certain
that God will meet me in my worst-case and make it not best-case
but blessed-case. Keeping that perspective is my secret to coping.

No Answer or the Wrong Answer

It's important to address that thing none of us in a waiting room of
life wants to acknowledge. Sometimes the answer we're looking for
doesn't come, or we get a different outcome than what we wanted.
Sure, there are times we made the problem bigger in our minds
than it really was. But there are situations that are truly as bad and
as big as we say they are.

God's delay in fixing the issues isn't because the circumstances are too awful or too hard—and we don't know why God chooses another path for us. I'm not one to promise you that we will get what we're waiting for eventually. Doctors still make mistakes. People still break our hearts. And death is always the final outcome of our time on earth.

What about our big God in those cases? Do those enormous problems negate God in any way? No way! Perhaps the bigness of God matters most when I don't get what I hope for. If he were a small, little-g god and he disappointed me, I wouldn't want anything to do with him. But he is the Lord God Almighty! Nothing is too hard for him, so if it doesn't come to pass, it's not because he failed. And he's not a cruel God. So, I will trust him, even if I'm stuck in the waiting room. He is here with me.

During the PAUSE

Pray

God, you amaze me with the way you take my needs and surprise me with your solutions. Your ways are higher than my ways. Let me never forget your goodness and your power.

Adjust

I will adjust my measuring stick to see God as bigger and my problem as smaller.

Undertake

I will quit justifying my misery and let go of my victim mentality as I wait for God to work out this problem.

Seek

I will seek God's provision, knowing his solution might be something I haven't yet considered.

Evaluate

I will evaluate whether I'm basing my emotions on my problem or on my Problem Solver.

QUOTE: "Don't tell God how big your storm is; tell your storm how big your God is!" –Unknown.

ME in the RAW: I know God is big, but where is he?

ME in the SPIRIT: My *big* God can do *big* stuff, and I'll see it when I get my *big* excuses out of the way!

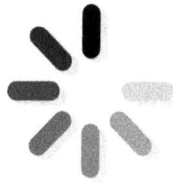

CONCLUSION

W here do you go from here? As you read this book, you probably unearthed situations awaiting answers. There were moments as you processed the PAUSE when the overwhelm intensified rather than eased up. Being in the messy middle comes with way more questions than answers, more problems than solutions. I hope you give yourself the benefit of grace in not needing to force a fix when it isn't yet time.

My prayer is that God's presence will comfort you and give you peace while you wait. And I'm asking God to nudge the people in your life to do their part to help you see some light at the end of the tunnel. So much of what we're waiting on depends on things outside of our control.

My heart is filled with concern for your situation. I'm in the trenches shoulder to shoulder with you. Sometimes it feels like we are in a battle, and we need a break. Other times it feels like nothing is happening, and we just want to do something!

As you ponder the takeaways from *Your Life on Hold*, I want to be sure you know I'm not guaranteeing a remedy will happen if you do these five quick steps:

1. Have more gratitude.

2. Have more faith.

3. Pray more.

4. Read your Bible more.

5. Tell others about Jesus more.

I've heard others promise a faith fix, and it's simply not true. Those actions are all well and good, but they aren't magical *get-out-of-jail-free* cards! Instead, hold tight. And when you can't hold *tight*, hold *on* to the hope that God is holding on to you.

&

During the writing of this book, I was diagnosed with a rare condition called Eagle syndrome. It is caused by elongation and calcification of a fang-like spike in my throat/neck area. It causes me to have a sore throat, neck pain, a change in my voice, an earache, headache, stiff neck, and an uncomfortable sense of broken glass in my throat when I sing. How fitting to be diagnosed with a disease with the word *eagle* in the term during this waiting period of my life. It reminds me of the waiter's verse:

> *But those who wait on the Lord*
> *Shall renew their strength;*
> *They shall mount up with wings like eagles,*
> *They shall run and not be weary,*
> *They shall walk and not faint.*
>
> (Isaiah 40:31 NKJV)

Here is another eagle verse:

> *Let all that I am praise the Lord;*
> *with my whole heart, I will praise his holy name.*
> *Let all that I am praise the Lord;*
> *may I never forget the good things he does for me.*
> *He forgives all my sins*
> *and heals all my diseases.*
> *He redeems me from death*

> **May I never forget the good things God has done for me.**

and crowns me with love and tender mercies.
He fills my life with good things.
My youth is renewed like the eagle's!

(Psalm 103:1–5)

We know there are times when physical healing doesn't happen until heaven. But there is still so much for which we can praise the Lord right now. During the next wait (and there *will* be a next time) may I never forget the good things God has done for me. More than that, may I not forget about God. I have that same prayer for you.

A Final Benediction

And now, dear brothers and sisters, one final thing. Fix your thoughts on what is true, and honorable, and right, and pure, and lovely, and admirable. Think about things that are excellent and worthy of praise. Keep putting into practice all you learned and received from me—everything you heard from me and saw me doing. Then the God of peace will be with you.

(Philippians 4:8–9)

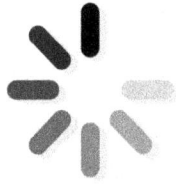

RESOURCES

List of Waiters (from the Bible)

- Joshua waited seven days for the walls of Jericho to come down. (Joshua 6)
- The Jewish nation walked in the wilderness forty years before coming to the promised land. (Joshua 5:6)
- After hearing about the flood, Noah spent a long time building the ark, gathering the animals, and boarding the ark. Decades. And then he spent almost a year on the ark waiting for the earth to be dry enough to deboard.[40] (Genesis 6–9)
- Sarah and Abraham waited past child-bearing years for Isaac to be conceived. (Genesis)
- In the New Testament, Elizabeth and Zechariah waited for their son John the Baptist to arrive. (Luke 1)
- All of Israel waited for the Messiah to come. (Old Testament and Luke 2)
- Mary waited through pregnancy for the birth of Jesus. (Matthew 1; Luke 1)
- Mary and Martha waited for Jesus to come to Bethany to help with Lazarus. (John 11)
- Paul waited until God opened the way for him to visit certain towns and people on his missionary journeys. (New Testament epistles)

- The disciples waited fifty days after the resurrection for the Holy Spirit to come. (Acts 2)
- Esther completed a year of beautification before her turn with King Xerxes. (Esther 2)
- Peter and the other disciples experienced empty fish nets before Jesus blessed them with full nets. (Luke 5)
- Job endured much loss. His life grew worse before it improved. (Job)
- David waited more than twenty years from the time he was first anointed by Samuel as king to the time he was king over both Judah and Israel. (2 Samuel 2–5)

> Patience is pumped up just like working a muscle during weightlifting—when it is tested.

How to Develop Your Patience Muscle

Patience is never more needed and never less present than when we are dealing with a time-out or pause. It's always best to develop patience ahead of time so that muscle memory shows up when you need it. Here are some tips.

1. Galatians 5 lists patience as a fruit of the Holy Spirit. That means it's up to the Holy Spirit to act in patience through us, and it's up to us to be yielded to the Spirit. What does it mean to be yielded or surrendered to the Spirit? It involves us being willing to follow his lead instead of the selfish desires that contradict Scripture.

2. Don't expect your circumstances to change. Patience is pumped up just like working a muscle during weightlifting—when it is tested.

3. Know that all human beings struggle with impatience, and

only a few learn to be patient during difficult times. It's easier to get frustrated than to have faith, and our go-to tends to be in crisis mode rather than choosing to be in Christ.

4. Patience needs to be stored up ahead of time for when you need it, and it gets depleted easily. Being in God's Word and talking with him in the good times banks spiritual fruit for you to have available during the bad times.

5. If you find yourself lacking patience, look through God's eyes of grace toward the situation or person frustrating you. This will allow you to put up with much more.

6. Sometimes the person you need to have patience toward is yourself. Grace yourself with forgiveness. Reduce your unrealistic expectations. Allow yourself more do-overs. Confess your flaws to God and ask him to transform your life.

7. When you realize that your purpose in life is so much bigger than this current circumstance, your ability to be more patient will flourish. Strive to look at the big picture—the kingdom picture.

8. Patience helps you trust God more. Trusting God helps you build more patience. They go together. When you have something to hang your hope on, you can wait with patience for all the details to be worked out according to God's purpose.

9. If you are a Christ follower, you are a temple of God, and conduit for the Spirit to flow through you. Patience moves unhindered through open conduit but is restricted when that conduit is plugged with pride and self.

10. When you choose to be impatient, you willfully refuse God's equipment to help you cope with your current situation. Patience is an act of obedience—evidence of a yielded, Spirit-filled life.

11. Practicing patience is not the same thing as stagnating. It doesn't mean you are complacent or compromising. It means

you are content in the wait but eager with hope for the next God-thing. It's not passive. Patience is active—acting on God's Word to stand your ground until he moves you on.

12. Patience gives you time to grow a more intimate relationship with the Father.

> Patience helps you trust God more. Trusting God helps you build more patience.

Bible Passages on Patience

James 1:2–4; 5:7
Colossians 1:10–12
Revelation 14:12
Philippians 1:6
Psalm 40:1

The Hebrew word in Psalm 40:1 for *waiting patiently* doesn't mean to be still or quiet. The word *qavah* actually means to eagerly expect God to act, and to be ready to spring into action when he does.[41] "It was not a single, momentary act of expectation or hope; it was continuous or was persevered in. The idea is that his prayer was not answered at once but that it was answered after he had made repeated prayers, or when it seemed as if his prayers would not be answered. It is earnest, persevering prayer that is referred to; it is continued supplication and hope when there seemed to be no answer to prayer and no prospect that it would be answered."[42]

For Your Bad Day

(This section was written during an eight-month waiting season. My husband and I were jobless, homeless, in a strange town, and living in a five-hundred-square-foot apartment waiting for whatever our *next* would be.)

Having a bad day? Try some of my remedies. Even though this is a bad time for my husband and me, it's not the end of the world. In each day, there's a way to celebrate life. We're on high alert for God's lessons and blessings. We try to season our bad days with joy. Maybe some of these will help you find joy on your bad days too.

- Laugh. Often. It's possible, even on bad days!
- Read God's Word and let him speak to you.
- Do something ridiculous and silly.
- Help someone.
- Play with your pet.
- Talk to God like he's in the room with you. (He is.)
- Drink in God's beautiful nature.
- Experience something new. New food. New place. New culture.
- Read a book outside your typical genre or style.
- Exercise and really push it. Don't go easy on yourself!
- Give someone the benefit of the doubt. (Including yourself.)
- Use your imagination. Create your own scenarios and conversations as you observe life around you.
- Dance like no one's watching. (And hopefully, they aren't!)
- Watch people. Grin at goofy-in-love couples and cute kids.
- Learn something new. Learning is the breath of life.
- Rest—really rest.

What can you add to the list? During a life pause, it's not about rewinding and rehearsing the painful circumstances. It's not about assigning blame. It's all about trusting God for what is yet to come and, because of that faith, having hope during the wait.

More Tips to Try While You Wait

1. Write a quote from this book or a Bible verse on a sticky note for a visual reminder.

2. Make an action plan from the "Put Off" and "Put On" list of Bible verses.[43]

3. Explore what the fruit of the Spirit means to you. (Galatians 5:22–25)

4. When you feel as if God doesn't love you, remind yourself that God loved you before you ever loved him. (Often, we feel unloved or unlovable when we are in a holding pattern, but God loves us no matter what.)[*]

5. Brush off any accusations or words of rejection.

6. Dwell in Christ. Dwelling on the what-ifs produces fear or doubt, which leads to being stuck. Dwelling in Christ leads to joy, which produces peace.

7. Shake off bad attitudes quickly and adopt a good God-attitude.

8. Write on a reminder card: "Nothing is too hard for God!"

9. Adopt gratitude and thankfulness to prevent or combat bitterness.

> You can help how you think, how you act, and how you wait things out. Change the way you think, and you'll change the way you feel.

---

[*] 1 John 4:19

A New Way

New reactions only happen when we first change our thoughts to the mind of Christ.

- Seek the mind of Christ (1 Corinthians 2:16).

- Meditate on God's Word. Start with Romans 12:1–2 in several versions.

- When we aren't in control of being on hold, we can choose how we think.

- Don't believe the cop-out that you can't help yourself. You can help how you think, how you act, and how you wait things out. Change the way you think, and you'll change the way you feel.

- We can turn away from thoughts that won't help us follow after God. We don't have to accept them. We can shake them off. Refuse the thoughts that cause us to be further from God. Substitute them with a God-thought.

- Will we self-destruct with our thoughts and feelings, or will we allow ourselves to be built up with healthy thoughts and feelings?

- Recognize distorted thinking patterns and deal with them. (Research this topic to identify the types of distorted thinking patterns you might be experiencing.)

- Imagine your unhealthy way of thinking is written on an Etch A Sketch and shake it away. Rewrite what you believe God wants you to think.

Seek Help

Sometimes, feeling stuck isn't a God-planned life on hold, but we need help getting out of it. I encourage those with struggles that are hindering their quality of life or disabling their activities of daily living to seek professional help. If you experience any of these situations, don't feel you have to go it alone. Make an appointment to discuss your problem with a pastor, counselor, physician, or other care provider trained in identifying and helping to alleviate struggles.

1. Mental health issues (depression, anxiety, bipolar, etc.)

2. Physical conditions (such as thyroid, menopause)

3. Unresolved relationship issues (abuse, infidelity, communication issues, control issues, etc.)

4. Disobedience to God's will, lack of repentance (either rebelling against his lead or blinded to it)

5. Fear (knowing God's nudge but afraid to move forward)

6. Doubt (unsure if it's God's voice or some other influence)

7. Ruts and routines (life feels like sleepwalking)

> Imagine your unhealthy way of thinking is written on an Etch A Sketch and shake it away. Rewrite what you believe God wants you to think.

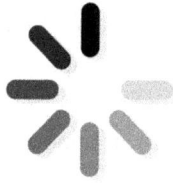

ACKNOWLEDGMENTS

I t seems my whole life has been one waiting room season after another. One thing that has kept me sane in the wait is the wonderful support of others. Here is my "grateful gratitudes" list of the ones who helped me with my waiting book and my waiting life.

Mom (Wanona Carlton). You waited nine months for me to get here and have spent a lifetime making sure I get where I need to go in life. Thank you for instilling in me the traits I've needed to be a better waiter. Endurance. Resilience. Perseverance.

My beta readers. Jessica Caudill, Julie Dahlin, Sally Ferguson, Lori Garza, Lisa McQueen, Mary Kay Moody, Pattie Reitz, Laurie Ritchel, Scherry Schneider, Robin Steinweg, and Joni Topper. I gave you a near impossible task, reading and commenting on the book, with just a month to get it all done. You highlighted the standout quotes and showed me which sections needed revisions. You cheered me on and prayed for me. Thanks for sharing how the book touched you in specific ways—it spurred me on. You helped me see how this book could make a difference.

WordGirls writing group. Because of words, we are family, and because of Jesus, we are sisters. Thanks for adopting me as your WordMama. You hold me accountable as I report in with each goal and progress report. I wish for you as many writing credits as you pursue!

My newsletter subscribers. Every time you open an email or watch a Grin & Grow video, you show me the work is not in vain. It's my privilege to use that "open" mailing list as a prayer list to offer boomerang prayers for you. See? It's not just about your praying for my ministry—it's an opportunity to get to support you in prayer too.

Joy Weese Moll, my writing buddy. Checking in with you every workday has been the top reason I can consistently be productive and work toward my goals. But it's not just about getting the job done. It's about the heart and mind connectivity that happens along the way. You've rooted me on during every stage of each book's life, from day one. You've seen me in the messy middle of each wait and lived it with me. Thanks for being in my life.

My wisdom team. You support me with your notes, calls, prayers, and wise words. If prayer had a waiting room, you'd be in it with me each time I have an on-hold season. Instead of feeling like I'm dwelling in the land of lull, because you check on me, I feel seen and heard. Special acknowledgment goes to Tammy Bokor, Jessica Caudill, Sally Ferguson, Stephenie Hovland, Becki James, Michelle Rayburn, Laurie Ritchel, Robin Steinweg, Sherry Schneider, and Dawn Wilson. Thanks for being in the trenches with me.

My countdown prayer team. The last two weeks before this book's deadline, I reached out to my friends and followers on Facebook to request prayer. I was blown away by the volunteers who signed up for a specific date to pray for me. You posted encouraging notes as I worked to complete the book. Your prayers made all the difference, and God, the One to whom you prayed, made it all possible!

My editor and book designer, Michelle Rayburn. Thank you for making my Grin Gal dreams come true. Your attention to editing details and clever design skills deliver a quality product every single time. I know career sense says not to mix friendship and business, but we seem to make it work, and I'm blessed that we can enjoy each other's company and companies!

My husband, Russ. When we said "I do," we had no idea the number of waiting rooms (figurative and literal) we would camp out in—and we don't even like camping! Thank you for sticking it out with me and being my rock, pointing me to Jesus, and quietly covering me with prayer. I know life isn't pleasant on the daily, but you make it a pleasure (even grin-worthy). I appreciate your patience when I get buried in book deadline details. How cool that the reward for completing this book was to spend our forty-first wedding anniversary together.

Triune God. Jesus Christ, my Savior and Lord. When I decided to follow you, I had no idea the journey would have so many pit stops, roadblocks, and detours. Those things would have still happened if I hadn't made you number one in my life, but your presence made all the difference. Holy Spirit, your indwelling equips me with the fruit of the Spirit, each one necessary to endure the wait. Your comfort gives me peace. Papa God, you tend to my needs as my Caregiver. Your strength is revealed through my weak spots. Your grace is sufficient for even these on-hold seasons. Use this book for your good purposes and glory.

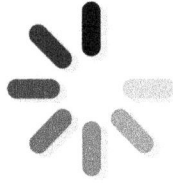

ABOUT THE AUTHOR

God's Grin Gal, Kathy Carlton Willis, writes and speaks with a balance of funny and faith, whimsy and wisdom. She coaches others to remove the training wheels of doubt and not just risk but also take pleasure in the joy ride of life. She is known for her debut book, Grin with Grace and for her grinning Boston Terrier, Hettie.

Not many funny girls also have Bible degrees! She graduated with honors from Bible college, holding degrees in Bible and church education, and served for thirty years in full-time church ministry with her pastor/husband, Russ. She's active as a book industry pro while also staying involved in her church.

Kathy works with women's groups and writers' groups, inside and outside of the church. She's passionate about helping believers have aha! moments with the daily application of Scripture.

Even with all the circumstances she's faced, she gives a clear message that she possesses an expectant hope and contentment in the Lord. Something we can all experience.

Kathy Carlton Willis owns KCW Communications, spinning many plates as writer, editor, speaker, and coach. Over 1,000 of her writing projects have appeared online and in print publications.

She is a contributing writer for *Upgrade Your Life, The Christian Communicator, The Christian Pulse, CBN.com*, along with others. Kathy also writes inspirational, motivational, and transparent posts and videos on social media. Subscribe to the Grin & Grow newsletter at her website to stay encouraged and in the know with all things Grin Gal.

Kathy founded WordGirls, a community of Christian female writers who receive professional coaching from Kathy.

She identifies issues that hold believers back, and her words illuminate their paths to freedom. Kathy reflects God's light during speaking programs as well as one-on-one counseling.

Learn more at Kathy's website: kathycarltonwillis.com

OTHER TITLES FROM 3G BOOKS

In addition to *Your Life on Hold: Don't Hate the Wait*, Kathy Carlton Willis has a full line of books. Kathy's boldly practical tips, tools, and takeaways show up in Christian living books, Bible studies, and devo-studies. 3G Books are perfect for small groups or individual reading.

The Grin Gal's Guide to Wellbeing: Being Well in Body, Soul & Spirit

Being well begins from the inside out.

This book is not just about Kathy's weight-loss and wellness journey. It's a guide for your pursuit of wellbeing. It doesn't provide a program for temporary behavior modification but a process for permanent God-led change.

On Kathy's quest for improved health, she discovered wellbeing is a balance of body, soul, and spirit. Her coaching style recognizes struggles, victories, aha! moments, and goals. She offers honesty, humor, and occasionally—homework!

The first section has chapters with the following features:

- Heartstrings (Stories)
- Heavenly Insights (Bible Study)
- Help Me! (Tools for Equipping)
- Homework (Making it Real)

- Health Check (Evaluation for Body/Soul/Spirit)
- Hurrahs and Happy Dances (Celebration of Victories)
- Hope Quest (Prayers)

The second section of the book includes practical resources. Join Kathy as a WellBeing Warrior. Activate personal stewardship by creating your own care plan using the tools of this guide. You won't always see a cure, but you can have a better quality of life.

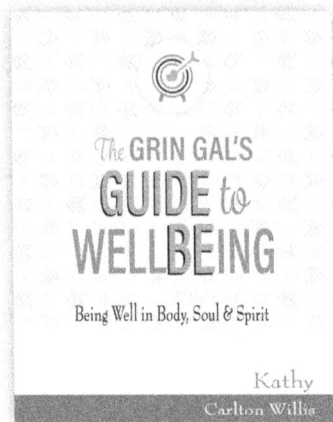

The GRIN GAL'S
GUIDE to
WELLBEING
Being Well in Body, Soul & Spirit

Kathy
Carlton Willis

Praise for the book:

Kathy's new book is a great resource for any woman looking to improve physical and spiritual fitness. Instead of presenting wellbeing as an ideal lifestyle to attain, she drives a better perspective—that God calls all of us to a life of stewardship.

–**Brad Bloom**, publisher, Faith & Fitness Magazine

Kathy writes with heart, clarity, and compassion about the struggles we face as we attempt to follow God's directions in taking care of our physical, mental, and emotional health. You'll walk away feeling encouraged and refreshed.

–**Sara Borgstede**, owner, Faithful Finish Lines
(Christian weight-loss programs for women)

The Grin Gal's Guide to Wellbeing identifies where you're stuck or struggling and helps you trust God to care for your soul and cultivate wellness in your physical, emotional, and spiritual life. With each page, you'll find inspiring stories and Scripture meditations, practical exercises, and laughs to lift your spirit!

–**Drs. Bill and Kristi Gaultiere**, psychologist (Bill) and therapist (Kristi), church ministry, authors of *Journey of the Soul: A Practical Guide to Emotional and Spiritual Growth*

The Grin Gal's heartwarming stories, practical homework, and heavenly insights will inspire you to grin on the inside. Everyone struggling with wise health choices needs to digest Kathy's practical insights in their journey to wellness and wholeness.

–**Charles W. Page MD, FACS.** Dr. Chuck is a speaker, author, surgeon, TV show host

The Grin Gal's Guide to Wellbeing is a perfect mix of inspiration and practical information. Kathy offers a holistic approach that is unique in the health and fitness industry and so refreshing! I highly recommend this book!

–**Karen Ferguson**, health coach, and the author of *Breath of Life: Living God's Promise of Peace*

I gravitate to stories that not only inspire me but also grab my hand and show me an attainable path. Kathy's immediate connection as a fellow struggler on the lifetime search for balanced health put me at ease and helped open my mind and heart to her specific suggestions.

–**Lucinda Secrest McDowell**, award-winning author of *Soul Strong* and *Life-Giving Choices*

The Grin Gal's Guide to Wellbeing is a practical resource that combines sensible strategies for health with biblical truths. My clients will benefit from the tools and motivational insights Kathy provides based on her own experiences of working through roadblocks to live a healthier life.

–**Cassandra DeWall,** licensed professional counselor at Praise Church

The Grin Gal's Planner for Wellbeing: A 90-Day Habit Tracker for Being Well in Body, Soul & Spirit

This 90-day habit tracker can be used in conjunction with *The Grin Gal's Guide to Wellbeing* book or separately. Customize the pages to fit what you need for your wellbeing journey. It is designed to help you grow in your personal stewardship. You'll find motivational quotes to fuel your wellbeing choices.

Pages offer guidance to include intentions that pursue wellness and wholeness of your body, soul, and spirit. This isn't just about weight loss or physical accomplishments. The inner being needs to be nourished and exercised too. Use the space as a planner or a journal—whatever works best to help propel you toward your goals.

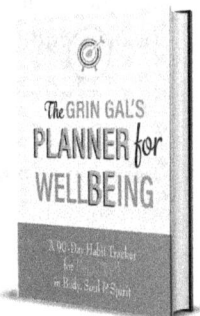

The daily pages have sections for food and fitness. You might want to use these as a planner to figure out your meals and exercises ahead of time. Or, if you prefer, use it as a habit tracker to document after the fact.

If you are creative, decorate the pages with colorful markers, doodles, tape, stickers, etc. If you are more of a bare-bones minimalist, use simple bullets to organize your space. Whatever works for you, put it to work for you!

7 Trials Every Woman Faces: Is Job a Member of My Family Tree?

Struggling with life challenges? You are not alone!

Ever wish for a friend who really understood you? *7 Trials Every Woman Faces* offers a virtual friend to lean on. Kathy comes alongside you as she shares insights learned through her own stinky situations.

All life trials fit in the same categories as Job's afflictions (told in the oldest book of the Bible). Whenever Kathy feels as if there's a "kick me" sign on her back, she asks, "Is Job a member of my family tree?" Laughing helps a little.

The chapter segments go along with the family tree theme:

- **Family Album.** Snapshots of heartwarming stories from real life.

- **Family Bible.** Biblical insights to overcome trials from a godly perspective.

- **Family Recipes.** Practical steps to help you grow and succeed God's way.

- **Family Legacy.** Lessons passed along as you help others endure trials.

Learn how to overcome Job-like trials when your family lets you down, friends misunderstand you, your health crumbles, your finances plummet, or others question your faith.

Everyone has trials, but it's the way we deal with hardship that determines not only the outcome but how we cope when we're smack-dab in the middle of them.

Praise for the book:

7 Trials Every Woman Faces is filled with wisdom. Kathy is an experienced guide who brings hope, help, and a ray of sunshine to brighten the rocky road you may be on. This book not only helps readers learn to cope but shows us how to help others suffering.

–**Pam Farrel,** author of 50+ books including bestselling *Discovering Hope in the Psalms,* co-director of Love-Wise.com

Incredibly practical and unfortunately relevant, *7 Trials Every Woman Faces* offers come-alongside wisdom, laughter, and plenty of application. Who knew Job could be so fun? Seriously, you'll giggle, grimace, and then shift to gratitude that you can work through this current batch of trials with a good friend.

–**Jane Rubietta,** international speaker and author of zillions of words, including *Brilliance: Finding Light in Dark Places*

This book is that companion you need to walk you through the trials of your present season. Kathy uses honest storytelling, humor, and solid theology to guide all of us on our Job-like journeys to a posture of hope.

–**Dorina Lazo Gilmore-Young**, author, speaker, contributor for DaySpring's (in)courage, Widow Mama Collective

With Kathy's uplifting stories and insightful Bible teaching, I believe *7 Trials Every Woman Faces* will become the go-to book for thriving in the midst of trials. Kathy walks readers by the hand through their struggles and gives them a new perspective. I especially like the section on difficult conversations. When you face uncomfortable situations head-on, you really can grin again!

–**Linda Goldfarb**, author of the *LINKED Quick Guide to Personalities* series, board-certified Christian life coach

The Grin Gal's Guide to Joy

If you've ever felt like the joy, joy, joy, joy down in your heart has gone missing, then this book is for you!

Kathy learned that happiness runs and hides, but joy remains when trials show up. Now she's here to share these principles with you in *The Grin Gal's Guide to Joy*.

In each chapter:

- **Grin with Joy** tells real-life stories and observations. You'll laugh at Kathy's humorous confessions and wacky insights.

- **Grow with Joy** features a joy word study and workbook. Kathy explores what the Bible says and unpacks timely truths.

- **Go with Joy** offers life application. Pick the action steps that help you live a joy-filled life.

- **Give with Joy** equips you to share joy and meet the needs of others. This is when faith becomes ministry.

- Your **Grin with Joy Challenge** describes a joy-challenging scenario to solve.

Praise for the book:

With her trademark honesty, warmth, wit, and humor, Kathy inspires us to grin with joy, regardless of our circumstances.

–**Christin Ditchfield**, radio host, speaker, and author of over 80 books

Kathy Carlton Willis writes stories from her open-book life in a way that makes me want to say, "She gets me! She really really gets me!"

–**Pat Layton**, author, *Life Unstuck*

With relatable stories of finding joy even in the challenges of life, Kathy leads the way with wonderful humor and refreshing honesty. Her joy is infectious!

–**Julie Zine Coleman**, speaker, author, and managing editor

Kathy is humorously serious about joy! She doesn't just tell us why we can grin with joy; she shows us how to go out and live joyfully.

–**Kathy Howard**, speaker, Bible teacher, and author

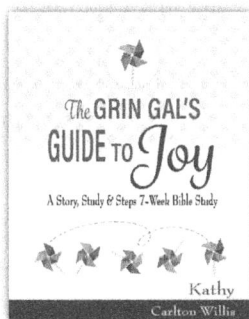

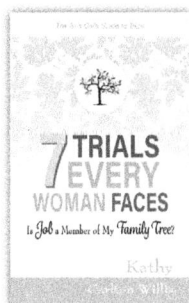

The Ultimate Speaker's Guide

The first book to kick off 3G Books was created with speakers in mind. Packed cover-to-cover with invaluable information, *The Ultimate Speaker's Guide* is the new bible for communicators.

With almost two decades of industry knowledge under her belt, Kathy Carlton Willis has coached hundreds of speakers to help them develop successful speaking businesses. This book covers all the tips, tools, and takeaways you'll need to ensure that your audience increases and your message is heard, including:

- Setting up your business
- Finding a brand that fits
- Getting more bookings
- Polishing your style
- Discovering God's plan for your business

An extensive resource section containing a sample contract, media interviewing tips, fee schedules, checklists, and much more, makes *The Ultimate Speaker's Guide* an essential toolkit you'll use time and again.

Praise for the book:

Whether you're new to speaking to promote the message God has given you or have been doing it for a while, you'll find a wealth of practical help in *The Ultimate Speaker's Guide*. Kathy's experience as a speaker and trainer fills a void in resources for Christian speakers.

–**Lin Johnson**, Former Write-to-Publish
conference director, 28 years

NOTES

1   Charles A. Beard, "Tendencies Affecting the Size of the Ballot," (Proceedings of the American Political Science Association, Vol. 6, 1909) 99, as cited in Quote Investigator, accessed August 10, 2022, https://quoteinvestigator.com/2015/01/19/stars-shine/.

2   Charles R. Swindoll, Laugh Again Hope Again (Nashville: Thomas Nelson, 2010), as quoted on Google, accessed September 15, 2022, https://bit.ly/3djuDA4.

3   Joyce Meyer, Battlefield of the Mind: Winning the Battle in Your Mind (New York: FaithWords, 2008), as quoted on Goodreads, accessed August 16, 2022, https://www.goodreads.com/quotes/405354-patience-is-not-the-ability-to-wait-but-the-ability.

4   Scott Pauley, "Are You in a Holding Pattern?" Enjoying the Journey (blog), accessed August 10, 2022, https://enjoyingthejourney.org/are-you-in-a-holding-pattern/.

5   AnnMarie Anderson, "How to Trust God's Timing" Busy Blessed Women (blog), May 25, 2020, accessed August 18, 2022, https://busyblessedwomen.com/how-to-trust-gods-timing/.

6   Elisabeth Elliott, Passion and Purity: Learning to Bring Your Love Life Under Christ's Control (Grand Rapids: Revell, a division of Baker Publishing Group, 2013), 61.

7   Bible Study Tools, s.v. "selah," accessed August 16, 2022, https://www.biblestudytools.com/bible-study/topical-studies/selah-meaning-in-the-bible.html.

8   Rick Ezell, "Sermon: While You Wait – Acts 1," Lifeway, January 1, 2014, accessed July 21, 2022, https://www.lifeway.com/en/articles/sermon-while-you-wait-acts-1.

9   Merriam-Webster.com Dictionary, s.v. "patient," accessed March 24, 2022, https://www.merriam-webster.com/dictionary/patient.

10 Elisabeth Elliott, Secure in the Everlasting Arms: Trusting the God Who Never Leaves Your Side (Grand Rapids: Revell, a division of Baker Publishing Group, 2020), 38.

11 Brittany Yesudasan, "How to Trust God, Even in Difficult Times," Cru, accessed August 18, 2022, https://www.cru.org/.us/en/train-and-grow/spiritual-growth/trust-god.html.

12 Joanna Smith, "When All Is Stripped Away," Fed and Fulfilled (blog), February 22, 2018, accessed August 18, 2022, https://fedandfulfilled.com/when-all-is-stripped-away/.

13 Andrew Murray, Waiting on God, (Abbotsford: Aneko Press, 2018), 06–07.

14 Charles R. Swindoll, Wisdom for the Way (Nashville: J. Countryman, a division of Thomas Nelson, Inc., 2001), 283.

15 Kathy Carlton Willis, Facebook post by author and responding comments, October 28, 2021, https://www.facebook.com/kathycarltonwillis/posts/10159350442789876.

16 Kathryn Shirey, "12 Things Truly Faith-Filled People Do Differently," Prayer and Possibilities (blog), May 24, 2019, accessed August 18, 2022, https://www.prayerand-possibilities.com/12-things-truly-faith-filled-people-do-differently/.

17 Karen Wingate, With Fresh Eyes: 60 Insights into the Miraculously Ordinary from a Woman Born Blind (Grand Rapids: Kregel Publications, 2021), 22.

18 C.S. Lewis, Mere Christianity, (San Francisco: HarperCollins Publishers, 2001), XV–XVI.

19 Original source unknown, Quote Investigator, accessed August 10, 2022, https://quoteinvestigator.com/2018/12/03/open-door/.

20 Rick Warren, "I want to change my circumstances. God wants to change me," Facebook post, May 16, 2012, accessed August 18, 2022, https://www.facebook.com/pastorrickwarren/posts/10150965415775903.

21 Shana Schutte, "With God It Gets Better," Wisdom Hunters (blog), June 30, 2020, accessed August 18, 2022, https://www.wisdomhunters.com/with-god-it-gets-better/.

22 Rick Warren, "You Can Worry, or You Can Worship," Crosswalk, November 7, 2015, accessed June 11, 2022, https://www.crosswalk.com/devotionals/daily-hope-with-rick-warren/you-can-worry-or-you-can-worship.html.

23 Kathy Carlton Willis, The Grin Gal's Guide to Wellbeing: Being Well in Body, Soul & Spirit (Beaumont: 3G Books, 2021), 165.

24 Rick Warren, The Purpose of Christmas (New York: Howard Books, 2008), as quoted on Goodreads, accessed August 15, 2022, https://www.goodreads.com/quotes/123181-the-more-you-pray-the-less-you-ll-panic-the-more.

25 David Platt, Radical: Taking Back Your Faith from the American Dream (Colorado Springs: Multnomah, 2010), as quoted on Goodreads, accessed August 16, 2022, https://www.goodreads.com/quotes/355341-radical-obedience-to-christ-is-not-easy-it-s-not-comfort.

26 Merriam-Webster.com Dictionary, s.v. "altar," accessed July 14, 2022, https://www.merriam-webster.com/dictionary/altar. A usually raised structure or place on which sacrifices are offered.

27 Merriam-Webster.com Dictionary, s.v. "lordship," accessed July 14, 2022, https://www.merriam-webster.com/dictionary/lordship. The authority or power of a lord.

28 Synonyms.com, STANDS4 LLC, 2022, "bolster," accessed July 14, 2022. https://www.synonyms.com/synonym/bolster.

29   Dianne Christner, "Seek Hope While Waiting," Wordserve Water Cooler (blog), September 22, 2013, accessed August 13, 2022, https://wordservewatercooler.com/author/diannechristner/.

30   Merriam-Webster.com Dictionary, s.v. "homesick," accessed March 24, 2022, https://www.merriam-webster.com/dictionary/homesick.

31   Katie Faris, "God Holds You On Your Hardest Days," Proverbs 31 Ministries, June 8, 2022, accessed September 14, 2022, https://proverbs31.org/read/devotions/full-post/2022/06/08/god-holds-you-on-your-hardest-days.

32   Melissa Kruger, "Three Truths About Contentment," Well-Watered Women Co., June 24, 2020, accessed September 14, 2022, https://wellwateredwomen.com/three-truths-about-contentment/.

33   J. Lee Grady, "God's Delays Are Not Denials," Places In The Fathers Heart (blog), July 1, 2010, accessed August 16, 2022, https://placesinthefathersheart.org/gods-de-lays-are-not-denials-j-lee-grady-3/.

34   Lysa TerKeurst, Unglued: Making Wise Choices in the Midst of Raw Emotions (Nashville: Thomas Nelson, 2012), 191.

35   Lisa McQueen, email, August 2, 2022.

36   Letitia Suk, Getaway with God: The Everywoman's Guide to Personal Retreat (Grand Rapids: Kregel Publications, 2016), 12.

37   J.I. Packer, Knowing God (Downers Grove: InterVarsity Press, 2021), 238.

38   Kathy Carlton Willis, Facebook post by the author and comments from consenting responders, August 24, 2013, https://bit.ly/3eU2yjt.

39   Lori Hatcher, "9 Reasons Why God Might Not Rescue You," Crosswalk, March 3, 2020, accessed August 18, 2022, https://www.crosswalk.com/faith/women/9-reasons-why-god-might-not-rescue-you.html/.

40   Mark Howard, "How long was Noah on the Ark?," Creation Ministries International, October 4, 2019, accessed July 22, 2022, https://creation.com/how-long-was-noah-on-the-ark.

41   Bible Study Tools, s.v. "qavah," accessed August 10, 2022, https://www.biblestudy-tools.com/lexicons/hebrew/nas/qavah.html/.

42   Study Light, s.v. "Psalm 40," accessed July 6, 2022, https://www.studylight.org/commentaries/eng/bnb/psalms-40.html/.

43   Blue Letter Bible, s.v. "put off," and "put on," accessed July 22, 2022, https://www.blueletterbible.org/study/misc/putoffon.cfm.

www.ingramcontent.com/pod-product-compliance
Lightning Source LLC
Chambersburg PA
CBHW051418090426
42737CB00014B/2726